# Defending Our Friend: the Most Hated Man in America

Mark & Sondra
Osterman ———————

# Defending Our Friend: the Most Hated Man in America

*The George Zimmerman We Know*

TATE PUBLISHING
AND ENTERPRISES, LLC

*Defending our Friend; the Most Hated Man in America*
Copyright © 2012 by Mark & Sondra Osterman. All rights reserved.

No part of this publication may be reproduced, stored in a retrieval system or transmitted in any way by any means, electronic, mechanical, photocopy, recording or otherwise without the prior permission of the author except as provided by USA copyright law.

The opinions expressed by the author are not necessarily those of Tate Publishing, LLC.

Published by Tate Publishing & Enterprises, LLC
127 E. Trade Center Terrace | Mustang, Oklahoma 73064 USA
1.888.361.9473 | www.tatepublishing.com

Tate Publishing is committed to excellence in the publishing industry. The company reflects the philosophy established by the founders, based on Psalm 68:11,
*"The Lord gave the word and great was the company of those who published it."*

Book design copyright © 2012 by Tate Publishing, LLC. All rights reserved.
*Cover design by Joel Uber*
*Interior design by Christina Hicks*

Published in the United States of America
ISBN: 978-1-62295-846-7
12.09.07

Dedicated to George & Shellie Zimmerman, We love you.

> "the friend who can be silent with us in a moment of despair or confusion, who can stay with us in an hour of grief and bereavement, who can tolerate not knowing, not caring, not healing, and face us with the reality of our powerlessness, that is the friend who cares"
>
> —Henri Nouwen

# Table of Contents

Introduction . . . . . . . . . . . . . . . . . . . . . . 9
Chapter One: That's What Friends Are For . . . . . 13
Chapter Two: Things Blew Up! . . . . . . . . . . . 33
Chapter 3: Hiding the Most Hated
    Man in America . . . . . . . . . . . . . . . . . 51
Chapter 4: Our Family's New Normal . . . . . . . . 71
Chapter Five: Who Are We? . . . . . . . . . . . . 95
Chapter Six: Headlines:
    Zimmerman Arrested and Jailed! . . . . . . . 105
Chapter 7: George Re-Arrested, Along with Shellie —
    Didn't Need That! . . . . . . . . . . . . . . . 125
Chapter 8: Is George Zimmerman a Racist? . . . 131
Chapter 9: Public Outcry Demanded George Be
    Charged…with Something . . . . . . . . . . 139

| | |
|---|---|
| Chapter 10: Closer Than a Brother | 157 |
| Photo Section | 173 |
| Postscript | 179 |
| Special Thanks | 181 |

# Introduction

*Mark Osterman's cell phone rang around 7:30 p.m. on Sunday evening while he and his wife, Sondra, were outside on a rainy evening walking their Rottweiler, Caesar. It was February 26, 2012. On the line was family friend, Shellie Zimmerman. Her voice shook as she blurted, "Oh, my God, Mark, George has been in a shooting! I am freaking out. I am headed home now. What do I do when I get there?"*

*The former infantryman and police officer, currently serving as a police officer for the Department of Homeland Security, told a frantic Shellie he would leave his home at Lake Mary as soon as possible to meet her at the gated community where she and her husband, George, lived. Lake Mary is roughly four miles from his best friends' house, which is located in The Retreat at Twin Lakes, an addition of town homes in Sanford, Florida. The two cities, Lake Mary and Sanford, sit side by side, and Mark Osterman has either rode, walked or biked over to the Zimmermans' countless times before. In fact, the families are so close; Mark keeps a key to the Zimmermans' front door.*

*After handing over Caesar's leash, Osterman darted back to the house to grab his car keys, shouting to his wife that he would call with an update as soon as he heard what had happened. He recalls clearly that it was raining when he pulled out of his driveway; easy to recall, because, before that night, the area had not seen rain in over two months.*

*Shellie's words, "George has been in a shooting," hung ominously in the air as he headed north on Rhinehart Road, but the seasoned veteran knew he would need to remain calm and offer support to George's wife who was clearly close to breaking down emotionally. While driving, he started to dial Shellie's number to get her location; she had been visiting her father across town. He had just started to enter her number when his cell phone rang in his hand. "Mark, I am losing it," Shellie said. "You need to help me understand."*

*"Shellie, tell me what you know about the shooting," Mark asked, hoping the brief assignment to report all she knew would steady her somewhat. She replied, "A neighbor called to let me know that George was involved in a shooting, but she said that George is okay. He is sitting in the back of a police car, but she could see George and it looks like he is okay."*

*It was not uncommon for neighbors to call George and Shellie Zimmerman. Often they would call George, the neighborhood watch captain, to report anything that seemed suspicious or of concern. They felt comfortable handing the information over to George and asking him to report to the police on their behalf. Later, when it would come to light that George made many calls to the police department before the night of February 26th, it would not be common knowledge that he was making most of those calls at the request of others.*

*From Rhinehart Road, Osterman took a right onto Oregon, the street leading into the Twin Lakes complex, and spotted Shellie's car already at the gated entry. She swiped her resident's card for entrance and the gate swung open allowing Mark to follow her inside. He then pulled in front of her to find a place to park a safe distance away from the site where the shooting took place. It wasn't difficult to find. There were more than eight police cars at the scene with lights rotating, fire emergency vehicles had arrived and neighbors had gathered in large groups, some carrying flashlights as they stood on the lawns in between the rows of townhouses. As a policeman for the sheriff's department, Mark had been on crime scene sites before, but this one was eerily different. As Mark and Shellie approached on foot, you could hear bits and pieces of the neighbors' conversations; whispers coming from out of the darkness as the steady rain continued to fall.*

*In the early hours of the morning following the tragedy, Mark Osterman would listen as his best friend, George Zimmerman, spoke in detail about the events that led up to the shooting of the unarmed teenager, Trayvon Martin; a shooting that touched off a firestorm of controversy, riveting and dividing our nation as questions were raised about racism, self-defense laws, and the power of the media who instigated a serious rush to judgment.*

*In the following pages of* Defending Our Friend: The Most Hated Man in America, *Mark and Sondra Osterman invite the reader to get to know the George Zimmerman they know; not the one demonized by the press as an out-of-control vigilante, or the one portrayed as the poster boy of the "right to carry" gun laws; but the George who stayed in the Ostermans' home during the weeks following the shooting while the Black Panther organization issued death threats and the intense media coverage threatened his safety and the safety of his family.*

*The Ostermans want others to know the mild mannered, caring friend who worked hard, enjoyed sports and cookouts, loved his wife, and treated the Ostermans' daughter as if she was his own. No one is better positioned than Mark and Sondra Osterman to offer this intimate glimpse into the initial shock of the event itself, the traumatic weeks that followed the shooting, then the unbelievable onslaught of negative press that took a weary toll on their dearest friend, George Zimmerman ... the most hated man in America.*

# Chapter One

That's What Friends Are For

*Mark*

As Shellie Zimmerman and I approached the yellow crime scene tape blocking off portions of a sidewalk and lawn inside the Twin Lakes community, we noticed a patrol car sitting a hundred feet away. Simultaneously, we realized it was George in the back seat, and he had seen us first. Then, he did a curious thing: he immediately ducked down and turned away, as if to lie down in the seat. Later, George would tell us what he was doing at that moment.

I nodded to several of the officers on the scene that night because I recognized them from ten years before, when I was a Seminole County Deputy in the area that includes Sanford, Florida. To one of the officers I said, "I have his wife here next to me; the guy in the police car. His name is George and this is his wife. Can you tell me anything that happened?"

The Sanford police officer quickly answered, "Oh, don't worry about it; from what I've seen, it's clean." This bit of "police jargon" meant, in the officer's opinion, it was pretty clear what had taken place since speaking to witnesses, and there weren't a lot of questions about the incident.

"So, what's going to happen with him?" I asked, pointing toward the car.

"We expect the violent crimes investigator to arrive shortly. After he gathers information here on scene, he will interview the guy down at the station. He will be held until we get all information gathered, then arrested or released, or maybe just held overnight. You can ask the investigator for further information; like I said, he's expected soon."

With those possible scenarios, I suggested to Shellie that we go to their place nearby and pick up a change of clothing for George. I knew if George was involved in a shooting, his clothing would be taken as evidence and examined for blood stains, gun powder residue, etc. He would need another set of clothing at the station. At this point, around 8:10 p.m., we had not seen the yellow tarp covering the body of Trayvon Martin, so we were not aware there had been a death as a result of the shooting.

I could see the anxiety in Shellie's face at the thought that George could be held overnight or even arrested. I tried to reassure her.

"Shellie, the most important thing is that George is alive and well. If he is arrested, we will work it out later when we get further information."

She methodically moved toward our cars and we left to gather the extra clothes. As we walked, I strongly encouraged her to pack a bag for she and George, so both would be prepared to spend the night at our home.

I offered our home for two reasons. If George was arrested or charged after questioning, I didn't want Shellie to be alone should she receive that word. I was also concerned for her safety. The shooting may have sparked anger in friends or family of the victim. I didn't want her to be by herself in their home, in case some person or persons sought some "street justice."

Fifteen minutes after we left the scene of the shooting, the patrol car with George in the back seat left for the short ride to the Sanford Police Station. The video of his arrival at the station would be played again and again as the public became aware of the shooting. To most, at first glance, George had no apparent injuries when he exited the patrol car. There was no visible bleeding or bruising; only one clip where an officer checks the back of George's head briefly. The video would unleash the first murmurings that the shooting could be more than a simple case of self defense.

As if in a fog, Shellie did the necessary things before she left their home in Twin Lakes for the night. I helped her walk their two dogs, an older Basenji named "Leroy" and their younger Rottweiler by the name of "Oso," Spanish for bear. Shellie then phoned her father and mother to give them the grim news. Of course, she was emotional as she recounted what she knew of the events that evening. I then waited while Shellie packed two separate suitcases; one for George and one for her. It was now around 9:20 p.m. when we pulled out of the gate in my Ford 2-door headed downtown to the Sanford Police Department on 13th Street.

Shellie and I entered the station and took seats in the lobby not realizing that we would be sitting there for the next six hours with absolutely no word about George. I watched Shellie go through a roller coaster ride of emotions. At times she was calm, even producing a smile or two as I tried to distract her from the heaviness. Then her countenance would change as fear gripped her once again. For Shellie, what we didn't know was worse than what we did know. Worry would often overtake her and fresh tears would fill her eyes.

I left Shellie's side briefly after calling Sondra to let her know both George and Shellie would be spending the night. Sondra had been ill that day and rather light-headed as a result. One of our dogs had been sick as well and had thrown up on the carpet. Sondra asked me if I could come home and clean the carpet if we were going to have overnight guests. She just didn't feel like she could do it. I rushed home, quickly cleaned up the mess on the carpet, and then changed cars for the trip back to the station. I thought our larger 4-door Ford Fusion would be more comfortable for transporting both Shellie and George.

My job remained one of comfort and encouragement to our friend during these long hours. Friends … best friends – that is what we called George and Shellie Zimmerman. I couldn't help but think of how my wife and I had become so close to this couple. So close, that we saw them as our younger brother and sister.

### Sondra

In 2006, I was working for First Trust Home Loans, a mortgage company no longer in business. I had thirteen years of experience in the business and my responsibilities included processing all loans. George Zimmerman was new to the mortgage business, but soon after joining our company, he became very successful. Since I processed the loans George originated, our daily interaction was important. He was eager to learn and we often discussed the mortgage business over lunch while getting to know each other and becoming fast friends.

George was a valued employee who treated each client with the upmost respect, even the really tough ones. He was producing on a consistently high level, which kept me extremely busy processing loans coming into the office due to George's efforts and others.

Our daughter, Breanna, was only four years old when she met George Zimmerman. Each day after school she would come to my office to wait until I was off work. While there, George went out of his way to get to know our little girl: talking with her on her level, treating her to snacks. Breanna thought she was George's personal assistant, and he allowed her to believe he "needed" her help to finish his work. Even as a four-year-old, Breanna would say, "Mom, Georgie is my very best friend."

I eventually introduced George to my husband, Mark, and they "clicked" immediately. They had many of the same interests. My husband, who is in law enforcement, enjoyed trips with George to the local shooting range for target practice. Mark and George often discussed the importance of protecting one's self and our homes and the importance of gun safety. They became inseparable, like brothers, even though George is fourteen years younger than Mark. Mark encouraged George to look into law enforcement as a more stable line of work because sales work has so many peaks and valleys. Mark thought George would be an excellent candidate for the field. With no military background, which is a distinct advantage when applying to work in law enforcement, George wanted to get some college behind him. He had been attending Seminole State College and working on a degree in Criminal Justice.

As Mark grew to know George better, he discovered for himself what I knew already. George is a kind man who would give away his last dollar, offer the shirt off his back to someone who needed it, and he is pleasant, sociable, and easy to be around. Mark and George also share a deep respect for women; neither can tolerate cursing or lewd, inappropriate behavior from men toward women.

It was in 2007 when George introduced me to his girlfriend, Shellie. Honestly, it was as if Shellie and I had known each other always. She is smart, kindhearted, and has a positive, bubbly personality. We went shopping together, met for lunch, and spent time talking over coffee at Starbucks. We formed a close friendship from day one.

I learned that George and Shellie had been friends for some time before they began a courtship. Their relationship moved very quickly and they wanted to get married as soon as possible. Mark and I could relate because we had a similar romantic story.

Because I was a certified notary public, George and Shellie asked me to officiate at their wedding and I was deeply honored. On a beautiful evening, November 17, 2007, we held the ceremony on Daytona Beach. The wedding was simple, but very intimate and sweet. I knew the two of them were meant to be together and I was so grateful that my friend had finally met his soul mate. I pronounced the couple man and wife just as the sun was setting, splashing the sky with glorious hues in the background. Later, those who attended the wedding met for a small reception, complete with the prettiest wedding cupcakes, then all went out to dinner to celebrate the new Mr. and Mrs. George Zimmerman.

We grew closer to the Zimmermans as the years passed; even spending vacation days and holidays together. Shellie and I enjoyed target practice as well, so we would accompany the guys to the shooting range or sometimes practice at my father's place in DeLand, Florida. My dad lives in a rural area on property that backs up to the Wekiva National Forest.

George and Shellie stayed busy. At one time both were taking college courses, plus working their regular jobs, but they always made time to hang out with us, and we enjoyed their company.

Earlier on the day of the shooting, Sunday, February 26, 2012, Breanna and I had been visiting my dad in DeLand, about thirty minutes away while Mark was working. By six o'clock that evening we all made it back to our home in Lake Mary. Mark and I were walking our dogs when Shellie called Mark's cell phone with the shocking news that George had been involved in a shooting at the Twin Lakes town home community where they lived. As Mark rushed off to meet Shellie he promised to let me know what was going on as soon as he understood more about what had happened.

I received a call an hour or so later from Mark, who was with Shellie at the Sanford Police Station awaiting news about George's possible arrest, or release. He let me know that Shellie, or perhaps Shellie along with George, would need our guest bedroom that night. The only information Mark had at that time was that George had evidently shot someone in self defense. At my request, Mark dashed home to help with a mess one of our dogs had made on the carpet. I had been sickly all day and didn't feel like I could clean it up, but knew it needed to be done before George and Shellie got to our place for the night.

After Mark returned to be with Shellie at the police station, I waited for further word, then at 12:30 a.m. I finally went to bed. I was not aware when Mark finally arrived back home hours later with George and Shellie. I would hear more details about the shooting from George himself the next morning around my kitchen table.

### Mark

At approximately 3:15 a.m. early Sunday morning, on February 27, following the shooting the night before, an officer entered the lobby to give Shellie and me an update on George's situation. We had been waiting there since 9:30 p.m.

"Mrs. Zimmerman, your husband is being released. He will be down in just a few minutes. He does have some injuries; a broken nose, several deep gashes to the back of his head," the officer said, giving us the first indication that George had been injured in the altercation. "I also need to let you know that the young man he shot has died."

The words hung there for a moment, then I heard Shellie gasp as she grabbed for a nearby chair and began to cry. I quickly came to her side.

"Shellie, it could be so much worse. George will be okay – he's alive, that's the good news."

The officer then added, "Mr. Zimmerman is getting changed and he will be released per the violent crime investigator. He will be coming down this elevator very soon." With that, he turned and walked up a flight of stairs off the lobby.

In an effort to lighten the mood, I said to Shellie, "Listen, you don't have permission to panic until I do. Okay?"

She tried to smile and answered, "Okay."

Fifteen minutes later the elevator opened and there stood George in the clothing that Shellie had brought for him. She went to him immediately. It was clear to Shellie, who was training to be a nurse and set to graduate from nursing school in the spring, George had been injured. She turned her husband around so that she could get a good look at his face. There was some bruising and cuts to his face and his nose was crooked and swollen; it appeared that the break was between his eyes, at the bridge of his nose. She turned him again to get a good look at the nasty cuts to the back of his head. Gel had been applied to seal the wounds and stop the bleeding to his face and head, but it was the look in George's eyes that I will always remember.

He was quiet, subdued, but stunned, almost as if in shock. I had seen victims of shock many times both in the military and in my profession. George had that look; the "thousand yard stare" that people get when they have seen too much, or been involved in traumatic events. He answered questions put to him, but did so while almost disengaged from the reality of the moment.

We listened along with George as the officer gave him the following information, "Don't leave just yet – we need to get your concealed weapon permit upstairs. Then, you'll be free to go. You can do anything you want, go anywhere, just make sure you call the detective once a day until the case is completely dismissed, or new evidence is revealed."

George nodded in compliance. Then the officer continued, "Your firearm will be kept as evidence. Now, there may be some media attention, but, you have the right not to speak to them – it's your call."

Of course, no one perceived that the officer's comment about "some media attention" would come to be the ultimate understatement.

The weapon permit was returned to George and he asked a simple question at that point, "You mean I could still carry a firearm with this permit?"

"Yes," said the officer simply.

"Wow," George responded softly, as if amazed there were no restrictions placed on him.

Then, Shellie and I flanked George as we walked to my car which was parked along 13th Street. I mentioned to George that we thought it wise for them both to stay in our spare bedroom for the night. I then, added, "And, we probably need to stop by the hospital and get you checked out."

He immediately declined the hospital stop, "I just want to go to your house and try to get some sleep. For some reason, I am bone weary and almost have to sleep right now." I understood.

For the next fifteen minutes while we made the drive to our home in Lake Mary, George recounted what he knew of the deadly encounter with the young black man; we did not know his name at this point. It was a story he would repeat for my wife, then his family, and other friends again and again. Each time he repeated the events of that night it would literally drain him, almost as if it taxed his very soul to remember those brief few frantic moments.

While he spoke from the backseat with Shellie, I saw him as my best friend, my brother. I had always been a mentor for George, but actually learned as much from him as he did from me. I hoped and prayed I could guide him through the tragic experience that had shaken him to his core. I pulled away from the police station, turned left on Southwest Avenue, then left again on Airport Boulevard before taking H.E. Thomas Road heading toward our home in Lake Mary. I listened closely as George told Shellie and me what happened that night:

"I left home on Sunday night to go do my shopping at Target. (George is hyper-organized and extremely thrifty, always following a budget. He went shopping weekly for dinners he and Shellie would share, and also purchased food for his lunches each day. He always packed a lunch to take to work. Shellie likes breakfast, while George doesn't, so she shops herself for any breakfast foods she prefers). I got into the car and started driving when I noticed this tall man, looking into a window of a residence. I was pretty sure he didn't live there, because I seemed to recall a shorter guy living there. Anyway, it is raining and it's dark and the guy is looking in the window. So, I stop under a street light to watch him for a moment. Then, I called the police on the non-emergency number to have them check the guy out. Well, the tall man sees me from about seventy feet away and starts toward me and he can see me under the light and knows I'm talking on my cell phone. While I'm talking to dispatch, the guy, who I now can see is a young black guy, is watching me make the call. He walks to the passenger side window and stands there a moment, then goes to the front of the car, comes around to my window on the driver's side, then toward the rear of my car, then walks away.

"I couldn't see him at that point. I didn't know exactly where he went. I am on the phone and the officer asked me, 'Do you still see him?' I said, 'No, I don't see him.' Then the officer says, 'If you can't see him, do you still need us to send an officer? We need you to get to a place where you can see him …'

(This is one of those points that will be important later: The policeman's direction to George can be interpreted different ways. Did George feel the officer was asking him to follow him in his car, or get out of his vehicle to see if he could see where the young man went? George chose the latter.) *"I'm walking outside in the rain still on the phone with the dispatcher when the officer says, 'Are you following him?'*

"I answered, 'Yes, I'm following him' … but I didn't see him, I am just going in the general direction of where I saw him last.

"The officer says, 'We don't need you to do that.'

"And I say, 'Okay.'

"The officer on the phone asked me where I wanted the responding officer to meet me and tells me the officer is almost on the scene, about 45 seconds away from the complex. I don't know the exact address where I am walking so I tell the dispatcher to just have the officer meet me at the club house. I put the phone in my pocket; turn around to head back to the car, when the guy is right there, fifteen feet away and walking toward me. He says, 'Do you have a problem?'

"I say, 'No, I don't have a problem.'

"'Well, you do now,' he says, and he's coming at me.

"I look down to get my phone, and that's when he decks me. I saw stars. The punch knocked me to the ground on my back. The guy jumps on top of me, straddles me with his knees up against my ribs and begins to beat me in the face, while my head is hitting the concrete sidewalk. When I tried to sit up, he begins to grab my head and smash it on to the concrete again and again, and I'm really afraid that I'm going to pass out.

"I notice that I'm about eight inches away from the grass, and I try to maneuver my body just enough to get my head onto the grass. About that time a man has come out of his house and I start shouting, 'Help me, help me!' The resident says he's 'not going to get involved' but that he would call the cops. I see another man and again shout, 'Help me, God, help me!" This man says nothing – just runs back into his house and I assume he made a call to the police as well. Two other men saw us out there and did nothing. I finally squirmed onto the grass, but then the guy on top of me takes one of his hands and puts it over my nose and pinches it closed while his other hand goes over my mouth. Afraid I was going to lose consciousness, I desperately got both of my hands around the guy's one wrist and took his hand off my mouth long enough for me to shout again for help.

"For a brief moment I had control of the wrist, but I knew when he felt the sidearm at my waist with his leg. He took his hand that was covering my nose and went for the gun, saying, 'You're gonna die now, motherfucker.'

"Somehow, I broke his grip on the gun where the guy grabbed it between the rear site and the hammer. I got the gun in my hand, raised it toward the guy's chest and pulled the trigger.

"The guy sat up and I heard him say, 'You got it, okay – you got it,' something like that. I am not sure what he meant, but then he pivoted ninety degrees and fell face forward onto the grass, and I scooted out from under him.

"I didn't know I shot him. I actually thought my shot went wide. In fact, I thought he might try to get up again, so after putting my gun back in the holster, I jumped on top of him and pinned his wrist on each side to the ground. A man approached out of the darkness, 'Are you the police?' I asked.

"'No,' the man answered. Then I could see another man emerging from the shadows with a flashlight.

"'Are you the police?' I called.

"'Yes, I'm an officer.'

"I think I said something like, 'Okay, good,' and I moved to my knees and the officer told me to put my hands on top of my head. He walked over and pulled my firearm out of my holster and then several officers showed up.

"The officers were bent over the young black man, who had not moved. Then, someone directed an emergency tech to look at my face and head while I was seated on a curb nearby. Another joined him, and they cleaned up my cuts, applying some gel to help stop the bleeding on my head. They inserted some gauze tubes into my bleeding nose, and taped some gauze pads to the back of my head.

"The officers were already talking to people on the scene about what they saw. I overheard one of the officers tell the medics, 'Clean him up good if I'm going to take him to the station. I don't want him bleeding on the inside of the car.'"

The last comment was probably not meant for George to hear. When he was telling us the story of the events that night, I understood what the officer was saying. After every shift, officers have to turn their assigned car over to the next officer on duty. It was his responsibility to make sure he handed over a clean and ready car. If it wasn't clean, the officer would have to take time to clean it himself. George continued:

"While they walked me to the car for the ride over to the station, one of the offices said, 'We think we have a pretty good idea of what happened here, but the detective is going to talk to you at the station.'"

The reason he had tried to duck out of our view when he saw Shellie and me approaching was simply because he didn't want his wife to see that he had been injured.

Then, George spoke about the hours he had spent being interviewed by the violent crimes investigator who focused on the same questions again and again. George said when the investigator told him the young man he shot had died at the scene, he cried. His strong Catholic upbringing taught him to value human life, and he felt deeply sorry for the loss of the young man and for his family. I looked at my friend and saw the weariness in his eyes, also the pain, and the confusion. From the moment I heard George speak about the shooting, I never once doubted that my friend was trying to survive that night just to make it back to his wife.

On the rainy evening of February 26, 2012, George felt his life threatened, and it was either him or the other guy; a young Trayvon Martin, a name everyone would come to recognize over the next few weeks. George Zimmerman would also come to own a fame he did not seek or relish in any way. In fact, in short order, everything dug up about George would be spoken of, written about, and discussed in every newspaper, talk show, and major news network from coast to coast.

All I felt for my friend was absolute heartbreak. I wanted him to know I would be there for the long haul, and said so before he and Shellie shut the door to our guest room that night; a night none of us will ever forget.

# Chapter Two

## Things Blew Up!

*Mark*

On the morning after the shooting, February 27, 2012, Sondra was up at 6:30 a.m. to get our daughter, Breanna, ready for school. After dropping Breanna off around 7:40, she returned to the house to find George Zimmerman and his wife, Shellie, seated with me at our breakfast table, making plans for the day. Sondra was shocked when she saw George for the first time since the altercation the night before at The Retreat at Twin Lakes, where George and Shellie lived.

George's eyes were black and blue, there were numerous cuts to his face, he had bandages on his nose and the back of his head, plus, he was moving very slowly from pain in his lower back. The ladies, in an effort to distract from "the elephant in the room," were talking about various topics while I tried not to stare at George. He sat to my right with both legs bouncing up and down nervously. With a pleading look, he turned to me and asked, "Mark, have you ever had to shoot someone?"

Although I had not experienced such an event personally, I had known fellow officers who dealt with the aftermath of shooting another human being. My father had such experiences, also, so I felt somewhat capable of guiding George through the emotional process. I knew his mental stability would depend on my encouragement, so I tried to assure him everything would be all right eventually and he would know a normal existence on the other side of this traumatic event.

George was going through the first phase of coping with the violent encounter of February 26th; he was in shock. We would also see George move from the shock of a traumatic event to the second phase, one of anger and confusion toward the person who caused him to react with such violence. Then came the difficult mourning period, when a deep sadness overtook George. No matter the details of an event, even one like this with a clear justifiable cause, there is still an overwhelming sense of guilt and remorse if you are the one responsible for taking a life; any life.

George's strong Catholic convictions were at play here, also. He felt he had committed an "unpardonable sin." I discussed this element with a pastor friend who explained the actual translation from Hebrew regarding the Old Testament commandment: *Thou shalt not kill*. He advised that an incident resulting in a fatality is not a violation of scripture if such an incident was justified and/or unavoidable. The Bible's recurring theme is that cold, calculated murder is prohibited and punishable, but one who is defending himself or protecting others is not considered a murderer. George was clearly doing what he could do to stay alive on the night of February 26th, 2012. Yet, he still grieved and was deeply sorry that the situation had cost a young man his life. Before long, his actions, even his motives would be questioned nationwide.

As we sat around the table that morning, we listened while George explained to Sondra what had taken place the night before. The information was exactly the same as he reported on the ride over from the police station. Once again, he repeated his fear that "he was going to die" during the deadly struggle and that the encounter was a "him or me" situation.

George told us about the moment he first learned the young man he had shot had died at the scene. He said he wept when he heard the news. He would not see the photos of Trayvon until the third and final interview with the police. As he spoke, Sondra and Shellie had tears in their eyes. We were feeling the emotional impact the shooting was having on George. His sadness was palpable as he spoke of the loss of "someone's son, or brother."

Both George and Shellie looked tired after a sleepless few hours, but George was actually trying to get around so he could report to work that day. We finally convinced him that he was in no shape to work, but he insisted on going to his office to tell his boss personally what had occurred, and to request a couple of days off to get himself together. I accompanied George to his office in Maitland, Florida, about ten or fifteen miles south of our home.

George's employer understood the situation, and he mentioned that George would need to be cleared medically before he could be allowed back at work anyway. From the office, I took George directly to be checked out by his primary care physician, and then he visited briefly with a therapist.

The medical doctor confirmed that George's nose was indeed broken. As for the lacerations on the back of his head, the doctor said the wounds should have been closed the night before; it was too late for stitches at that point. The doctor also indicated the lower back pain George was having was likely due to a sprain or strain of the sciatic spine and ordered him to take it easy for the next several days. George was granted a leave of absence from his job citing Post Traumatic Stress Disorder (PTSD). He would need to recover physically and mentally from the events of Sunday night, February 26th.

George received word the police would have follow-up questions for him later that afternoon. He was to report to the Twin Lakes subdivision at 3 p.m. to do a "walk-through," a reenactment of the shooting. I tried to assure him the police were just following procedure and that he needn't worry. "Just keep telling them the truth, that's all you can do."

### Mentoring George

Let me take this opportunity to describe a little more about the relationship between George Zimmerman and me. From the time we met, I knew there was a possibility I would enjoy a strong, lasting friendship with the man. I realized that George was looking to me for advice in several important areas of his life. I don't know how qualified I am to be anyone's mentor, but, when George sought me out on any topic, I tried to respond and offer sound counsel to my young friend. As often happens, in a mentoring relationship, I learned a great deal from him, too, as our friendship grew.

George expressed disappointment over some of the decisions he made in his younger years. Who doesn't wish they could go back and change or erase some of the stupid things they did in high school, or college? One of the biggest changes I saw in George due to my direct influence was his use of alcohol. He went from being a casual drinker to nearly removing drinking from his life totally.

I came up with a term years ago for people whose lives center around drinking and frequenting bars; I call it living in an "incessant haze." It is a cycle that moves from getting drunk, dealing with the hangover, then recovering from a weekend of clubbing or partying, only to repeat the entire cycle the next weekend. I told George the "incessant haze" is an alcohol-induced lifestyle that saps you financially, compromises your integrity and decision-making ability, ruins your reputation, and is a total waste of time. I encouraged George instead to embrace "cumulative clarity." The term I came up with refers to the mental and emotional state of people who refrain from alcohol use and are in control of their faculties at all times. It is a choice one makes to reject booze and partying, along with the sleazy trappings of frequenting bars and the compromising situations in which one can find himself. George took to heart what I said and began to cut his drinking down to an occasional glass of wine or beer. I was proud of him for making that kind of mature decision.

I also think I had something to do with George's desire to manage his finances as he and Shellie found ways to become more frugal. They began to shop wisely and became adamant about saving money. In fact, with the additional money saved, they became involved in the "Big Brother/Big Sister" organization. The couple was assigned two African American children of a single mom; the father of the children was incarcerated. George asked me often about how he could better direct and encourage the children. The best advice I gave him was to refrain from "preaching" to the kids about studying, or about their choice of friends. I told him to calmly approach such subjects and always be eager to affirm any good decisions or efforts the kids made. I also told him to keep progress reports to a short time frame; don't set goals too far in advance. "Check to see how your kids are doing on a week-to-week basis, instead of hitting them up for grade and conduct reports after a full semester."

George and Shellie rewarded the kids' good grades and behavior by taking them to basketball games, movies, bowling, and their favorite restaurants. Mainly, the children knew the couple was there for them and that they would listen and care about their problems, their hopes, their dreams. The children came from a depressed neighborhood so the time spent with George and Shellie had a positive, consistent impact. Not only did George and Shellie love these two kids, they also respected their hardworking mother who was extremely grateful for the time the couple spent with her children.

Later, when the story of the death of Trayvon Martin hit every newsstand coast to coast, George understood how difficult it would become for the mother of the two children he and Shellie mentored, should she speak out in his defense. She would have been subject to extreme hate and hostility within her own neighborhood, so he insisted she remain silent for her own safety. The woman reported to George however, that she and her whole church family were praying for him daily. She said to George, "I know you are not the person the media has made you out to be."

When the media frenzy first began, George and Shellie asked an African American couple, one of whom he worked with, to take over their mentoring duties. George and Shellie didn't want his volatile situation to adversely affect the kids. The black couple agreed to step in and become involved with the children while George faced on-going scrutiny and possible arrest.

George also turned to me often for advice about his relationship with Shellie even before they married. He had known Shellie for two years, but they had only been dating a short time after we became friends with George. Now they were considering marriage. George observed how Sondra and I interacted and expressed on several occasions how he yearned for the same kind of satisfying relationship. As I became closer to George, along with police work, we discussed every aspect of married life. I think the greatest piece of advice I gave him in that regard was my Rule #1 regarding communication: *Never Raise Your Voice.* Yelling at someone only makes the person you are yelling at want to get louder than you. Long-term stress and frustration are the only dividends from this strategy. George's response to this point was a simple question, "What if *she* is the yeller, not me?"

I understood the question because I had married a lovely, but quite vocal lady, myself. Early on, my Sondra often raised her voice in heated discussions, and I knew for the sake of marital harmony there had to be some changes made. We agreed on a new rule for communication: whoever raised their voice during any discussion lost the debate instantly. Of course, it took some time for the rule to become second nature, but it worked. It worked so well, our eleven-year-old daughter has never heard her mother and father raise their voices at each other.

I remember one particular visit I made to the office where Sondra and George worked. George met me near the front door and we gave each other the customary "brother hug," then George noticed how my face lit up when I saw Sondra walking toward us. "Hi, girl," I offered.

She responded with a big smile, "Hi, baby," then continued on to finish some office task. George turned to me and said, "That right there is what I want. You see her every day, yet, you're still happy to see her each time." I simply nodded and smiled in response.

Another re-occurring topic of conversation with George was the importance of establishing lifelong habits. I truly believe we *are* the habits we indulge. For instance, I shared with George how important it was to establish the habit of remaining calm in all situations. It's my opinion that a person can create and exist within their own "peaceful zone": a place where others feel welcome and safe, too. George bought in to this concept and was eager to develop his own inner calm, one that would benefit him in every situation.

I hope the reader has a good feel for the relationship existing between George and me. I knew George was learning from me and depending on me to be forthright, open and honest about what I had learned from life, but, as stated, I had great respect for him as well.

## Follow-Up Interviews at the Sanford Police Department

George had been questioned briefly at the scene inside the town home community at Twin Lakes, in the moments following the shooting of Trayvon Martin. From police training, I knew these preliminary questions may or may not have been done with Miranda Warning Rights stated, depending on the type of questions asked.

Some general questions are necessary to secure a crime scene. First, the crime scene perimeter is established, then statements are taken from witnesses. There is a search for evidence with the officers making sure to protect or preserve any evidence discovered. Traffic control or crowd control may be necessary to assist medical personnel as they arrive on site. The officers also keep a keen eye out for possible trouble from friends or family members of the victim or perpetrator. After preliminary questions at the scene, George had spent hours at the police station answering questions and going over the details of the deadly encounter. He was a bit concerned about further questioning scheduled for Monday afternoon. "What else could they possibly ask me?" he asked.

Again, I told George the detectives were only doing their job, and he needed to cooperate fully. At this point, he hadn't even considered the possibility he would need a lawyer.

Before noon that Monday morning, George and I had made visits to his office, his doctor, and he spoke briefly with a therapist. Then, a few minutes before three o'clock that afternoon, I drove him over to his townhome at Twin Lakes to meet up with his father, who wanted to be there during the questioning. As we pulled on to George's street, we noticed Mr. Zimmerman sitting in his car in front of the townhome where George and Shellie lived. The decision was made earlier that I would drive George over to the scene, because the police indicated he could be arrested following questioning that day.

Sanford police detectives arrived and informed George they would walk with him over to where the shooting took place, and that he would be video taped as he described the events of the night before. They said, "Every word, every gesture, every step will be recorded and could possibly be used as evidence in the case."

Mr. Zimmerman and I kept our distance, standing forty or fifty feet away from the camera at all times while George pointed out where he first saw "a young tall black man who was acting suspiciously." He explained how he exited his car to see if he could determine where the young man went while on the phone with the non-emergency police contact. George offered details of the struggle once more, including how he had called out for help several times.

We could see the strain on George's face as he went to the ground to demonstrate the position he was in when he felt Trayvon going for the gun George carried at his waist. It was emotionally draining for George as he relived that awful moment when he managed to control the gun, then fired out of fear for his life. The camera rolled until George had nothing else to add. Once more he had told them everything.

After the reenactment, the detectives asked George to return to the police station for further questioning. They also asked if he would volunteer to take a voice stress test. Without hesitation, he agreed and climbed into the patrol car for the trip over to the Sanford Police station.

Most people are familiar with polygraph testing (lie detector tests), but the voice analysis procedure, developed more recently, is considered more accurate than polygraph tests. Neither is admissible in court, but the premise is basically the same for both: an individual's pulse rate increases when he makes a decision to lie; not necessarily while they are speaking, but just before. Like the polygraph, an administrator starts by asking ten or more general questions like, "When is your birthday?" "What did you have for breakfast?" "What is your mother's first name?" As the questions change to become crime related, the computer is so sensitive it can tell if the individual's answers waver at all from the earlier general responses.

After the examination, the police informed George that he passed the voice stress analysis test. I think it also went to George's benefit that he was so willing to take the test. He didn't "lawyer up" or try to evade the request. The reason was clear; he was telling the truth.

He was called again Monday to the station for further questioning and yet again on Wednesday. Whenever George left for additional questioning it was extremely difficult for all of us, but especially for him and Shelley. We were never sure if he would be arrested or be allowed to return home following each questioning session.

George presented himself for another examination for the purpose of determining if it was George or Trayvon Martin calling for help during the struggle on the evening of February 26th. These voice analysis tests were conducted by the Florida Department of Law Enforcement (FDLE), not the Sanford Police. I remember this was the beginning of March, around the time we heard about the first protest rally organized by Reverend Al Sharpton.

Sensitive audio equipment was set up at a facility by the FDLE here in Sanford. When in place, they asked George to lie on his back and scream out for help as he did on the night of the shooting. From my experience I knew a 75% match would hold up in court; to get a 100% match they would have needed the *exact* weather conditions and the actual cordless phone used to make the call. He was later informed that the test confirmed (by a 90 to 95% match) it was indeed his voice heard calling out, even though Trayvon's mother insists that it is her son's voice heard on the 911 calls.

The questioning by the police grew more intense with each session. The last time George was questioned was on the Wednesday following the Sunday incident, and it was brutal. I understand the intent; detectives have to see if a subject is going to change his story in any way. George held up under the barrage of questions that included attacking his every word uttered since the shooting. He was exhausted and visibly shaken after being hammered for hours. "I can't believe it, they don't believe a word of what actually happened?" he said on the drive home.

George told me how the investigators tried to trip him up by lying about evidence, stating there were issues with his story, interjecting half truths, bullying him into changing his account of the shooting. At one point they told

George, "Knock off this foolishness and just tell us what we already know from the evidence." I knew this was their job and if they could catch him in one lie, it would be enough. The only way to withstand such relentless attacks was to continue to tell the truth.

This interview was difficult also because for the first time he heard the 911 calls made, recording his calls for help, which forced him to relive that terrible night all over again. He said he "teared up" when shown the photos of Trayvon, lying dead on the grass. At one point, he became so upset with emotion, he vomited during the interrogation. He was still suffering with nausea and threw up later after he returned to our home. He was a wreck.

To keep George calm, I explained the process as I knew it. "Unlike you, there are criminal types that lie about everything. I have observed interviews conducted by men who have mastered techniques to produce a confession or catch the suspect with irrefutable evidence. Everything from the 'bad cop'/'good cop' routine to full-out verbal, almost physical aggression is used to try and shake the suspect's account."

I was kicking myself for my decision to send him in to the interviews without giving him a little more advice. Later, I would be accused of coaching George for the interviews. That was totally false. I realized that if I had tried to warn him of the different questioning methods, he may have focused on sidestepping the assaults rather than just speaking the truth as he knew it. He did so, again and again.

I kept telling him, "If they had evidence to arrest you, they would have done so already." But he couldn't shake a constant, nagging fear that told him they were not going to let this go. Turns out, he was right.

While George was trying to cooperate fully, a storm of controversy was just beginning to brew, stirred first by local media who latched on to the story, spinning the details to suggest this was a racially motivated incident; an event of racial profiling that ended in the murder of an unarmed teenager, Trayvon Martin. None of us were prepared for the media frenzy to come, nor were we prepared for the venomous outpouring of hatred toward George.

# Chapter 3

## Hiding the Most Hated Man in America

*Mark*

Although I consistently tried to encourage George, I, too had a foreboding, perhaps based on years of experience in law enforcement, that the incident on February 26th at The Retreat at Twin Lakes housing addition was not going away anytime soon.

By Thursday, March 1, the local Orlando press had jumped on the story, and like a break-away avalanche, newspapers, magazines, and talk shows around the country began to clamor for more details. Because of the way in which the story was presented from the beginning, the racially charged elements had people picking sides quickly.

Even though the Zimmermans and Sondra and I didn't realize the extent of the media coverage at the time, we all agreed from that first night to tell no one the couple was staying with us. George and Shellie's parents and siblings were the exception, along with the Sanford police, of course. Not even Sondra's extended family, nor mine, knew we were keeping the Zimmermans during those first hours and days following the shooting of Trayvon Martin.

I would recall the words of the officer from the Sanford Police Department after George's first interview at the station. "There could be some media attention in the coming days, however, please remember, you do not have an obligation to talk to anyone." I knew he was advising that speaking to the media might only create more fodder for the newspaper or news outlets hungry for details. So, we agreed to "lay low," to not be seen or heard, optimistic that the press interest would die down eventually and we could get back to our normal lives soon. What a field day the press would have had if they knew George Zimmerman, the focus of the biggest story to come out of Sanford, Florida, was staying with friends only blocks away from the scene of the shooting.

During the month leading up to the shooting, George's grandmother, whom he adores, had been hospitalized. Up until then, he had not been in close contact with his brother in Washington, D. C., or his sister and parents who now live in the Orlando area. Concern over their grandmother's illness, however, brought the Zimmerman family together. A level of respectfulness was restored to George and Shellie during his grandmother's medical crisis and an overall pleasantness between family members ensued. George was very grateful for the good, healthy relationships he was once again enjoying in the days leading up to the incident at The Retreat at Twin Lakes. Later, he would be disappointed with some of the decisions his family made; mainly how they spoke to the media against his wishes, but he loved them very much and needed their support during those hard days.

Then it got crazy. Soon, every news report included new details of the case and speculation as to where George Zimmerman was. He and Shellie's home at Twin Lakes was being watched around the clock. Neighbors were hounded for information. Former workers and classmates of George, even distant acquaintances, were being questioned about the character and motivations of the man accused of shooting to death seventeen-year-old Trayvon

n. Rumors were rampant as the press began to demand more and more information.

The photo of George released to the public was a mug shot taken in 2005 when he was 21 years old. Yep, George has a record. The picture shows an overweight George sporting a scraggly beard, unshaven and disheveled. That photo doesn't look at all like the 29-year-old George today. He has dropped the extra weight, is clean shaven and in very good shape.

The arrest in '05 was for "battery on a law enforcement officer and obstructing justice." The police report says George walked up to a friend who was being arrested near the University of Central Florida. He was talking to the friend and refused to leave when a plain clothes officer instructed him to do so. The arresting officer said George cursed at him, then instigated a brief shoving match. Since it was his first offense, George paid a fine and took anger management classes, and the charges were dropped. In a letter explaining his actions, he claimed the officer never identified himself. "I hold law enforcement officers in the highest regard as I hope to one day become one. I would never have touched a police officer."

George and I talked about this incident early on in our relationship. He still didn't recall the officers identifying themselves. They reported that they had done so. Still and all it wasn't the smartest thing to do. He agreed.

The mug shot helped to form the public's opinions of George, while photos of a young Trayvon, smiling innocently from under a gray hoodie appeared next to every story. Some accounts included pictures of an even younger Trayvon, playing Pop Warner football or Little League baseball.

Some newspapers were reporting that Trayvon Martin was shot by George Zimmerman, a "white man." The irresponsible error got black communities even angrier. Then, media started referring to George as a "white-Hispanic." What is that? George's father is white and his mother is Latina (born in Peru). George himself is neither dark-skinned or light; he's sort of light brown. Of course, on the dark, rainy evening of February 26th, he could have been green and the outcome would have been the same.

Erroneous, exaggerated reports of "racial profiling" stirred a tempest that spread like wildfire across the country. A report accompanied by a grainy video released by ABC showed George arriving at the Sanford Police station following the shooting with no visible signs of a struggle. He was shown easily exiting the police car and walking unassisted into the station. There was no apparent blood, cuts or noticeable abrasions or bruises. From that video, most people would doubt that George had been involved in a life-or-death struggle. Later, after public outrage, it was determined that ABC failed to release information that George had been treated for cuts and lacerations at the scene. They also failed to air the part of the video that shows an officer stopping to check the cuts to the back of George's head just before he entered the station. The network apologized for previously reporting George had no apparent injuries. They then aired the enhanced video images showing clearly the deep scrapes to the back of his head and facial injuries. But, the damage had been done.

NBC News also mishandled the broadcasting of the 911 call George made to the police dispatcher on the night of the shooting. The call was edited in such a way that insinuated George was racist. The edited audio seems to have George saying, "This guy looks like he's up to no good (a brief pause, then) … he looks black." This edited clip suggested that George targeted Trayvon because he was black. The actual call reveals George stating, "This guy looks like he's up to no good. Or he's on drugs or something. It's raining and he's just walking around, looking about."

The 911 officer responds, "Okay, and this guy – is he black, white or Hispanic?"

"He looks black," George replied in direct response to the officer's specific question. It is alarming how statements can be twisted or manipulated to mean many different things.

Even the funeral director who received Trayvon's body to prepare for burial added to the debate. "There were no physical signs like there had been a scuffle," said Richard Kurtz. "The hands ... I didn't see any knuckles, bruises, or what have you, and that is something we would have covered up if they had been there. He looked perfectly normal to me when he came in, and the story just does not make sense that he was in this type of scuffle or fight in anything that we could see ... except, for the gunshot wound." These statements and others fueled deep suspicion that George targeted Trayvon from the onset.

By the weekend, we knew that keeping George hidden was not only a wise decision, but could possibly save his life. Just before Trayvon Martin's funeral was held on March 6th, a group calling itself the New Black Panther group issued a death warrant for George, offering $10,000 for his life. The head of the NAACP, Ben Jealous, also stated during a nationally televised news conference that the "KKK was alive and well in Sanford!"

Because no arrest had been made in the Trayvon Martin case, the Sanford Police Department came under heavy fire. Soon there was a national movement, calling for George's arrest. In particular, the Chief of Police for Sanford, Billy Lee, took the heat for what many were calling "a bungled investigation." Coffee break conversations and random comments included: "They didn't even do a gun powder residue test on the guy"; "Can you believe they handed Zimmerman's gun permit back to him?"; "Hey, the crime scene wasn't even protected"; and, "You know, because the kid was black, the police determined it was a case of self defense and never even looked at other possibilities." Political pressure was placed on city officials to remove a good man and a great officer, Chief Lee.

I personally detested the attacks against Police Chief, Billy Lee. We had a connection that went back at least ten years. He rose through the ranks and was once my road patrol lieutenant for the Seminole Sheriffs Department. I love my father, but often do not relate to him. Dad is like a sledge hammer viewing every problem, even the smallest ones, like a nail he has to beat down to win. I came to know other men, like Chief Billy Lee, who personified wisdom and genuine concern. His priorities included fairness and compassion when dealing with problems and people. Billy Lee was a man of great character. He didn't have to say anything to communicate. When things needed to be done, he had a certain look that let you know he was expecting the best from you.

Some were calling for the Chief's resignation days before the 911 tapes were released to the public. So, even before evidence was examined and processed, political pressure from the top down was being applied. The black community threatened riots and other repercussions because George Zimmerman had not been arrested. The blame was squarely placed on a good man, a respected police officer who had only been in the position for ten months. Chief Billy Lee was finally forced to step down. It was sad. By the end of June he would be terminated.

In the days leading up to and following the funeral of Trayvon Martin, marches were organized across Florida and then spread to other cities all around the country. Signs, t-shirts, posters were printed for the marchers. A threat of racial violence was chosen as a motto: No Justice, No Peace. Even the hoodie Trayvon was wearing on the night he was shot became a symbol against racial profiling. Seems everyone was donning a hoodie: Congressmen, NBA basketball players, movie stars, politicians, thousands of kids marching in protest. "I am Trayvon" rallies and demonstrations were organized and covered by news media from coast to coast. George followed news of the protests in amazement and always with an unsettling, unshakable fear.

While the world was asking, "Where is George Zimmerman?" we tried our best to move through the days without becoming caught up in the fear and confusion emanating from the negative outpouring and very real hatred toward George.

I never dreamed it would be possible in America that a family would be prisoners in their own home because people presumed a man "guilty" before any evidence was presented, before an arrest or trial. I knew I was prepared to defend George, Shellie and my family should anyone approach our home intent on doing harm. I just never thought it would actually become a very real possibility.

During these tough days, George insisted that Shellie continue nursing school. She was set to graduate in the spring, and he wanted to make sure she stayed on track there. So she left for school each day while I reported to my job as usual. It is to their credit that none of the supervisors, instructors, or fellow nursing students divulged Shellie's identity to the press. Breanna went to school every day, and she understood how important it was to keep George's whereabouts a secret. Sondra was not working at this time.

George spent the days in our home making copious notes; detailing what specifically he recalled about each moment of the encounter with Trayvon Martin. He watched television and would become confused and depressed with the onslaught of negative coverage. In between, he had bouts of extreme fear for our safety.

The only time he ventured out of the house was in the late evening. He would sometimes wear a hat, even sunglasses to walk his dog. It was a much-needed reprieve because George loved to be outdoors. The streets of our Lake Mary neighborhood are relatively quiet and there are few people out after 9 or 10 p.m., so he would walk and think mostly about the future. His emotions would swing from confusion to depression to concern for all of us, day after day.

*Sondra*

Toward the end of that first week following the shooting of Trayvon Martin, Mark and I thought it would be nice for George and Shellie to get away from the stress for a little while. We helped to make plans for them to drive to Tampa, stay in a nice hotel, relax and truly get some rest. We were all very naïve to think that when they returned everything would have blown over and the media would move on to another story. We really believed that soon George and Shellie would be moving back to their home to get on with their lives. We could not have been more wrong.

The media firestorm surprised all of us. I bristled at how the media got the details of the events from that February night so wrong; it seemed like the driving force of the misinformation was the attorneys for the Martin/Fulton family (Fulton is the last name of Trayvon's mother). The family was demanding answers regarding the death of their son, and they deserved answers. However, during their quest for answers, they racially divided the country by baseless accusations. The outcome left people confused, and seeking justice for suspicions based on lies and hate.

We couldn't escape the press coverage. The shooting was the lead story for every newspaper and magazine. Every news show featured segments and updates on the Tryavon Martin shooting in Sanford, Florida. We caught the television footage of the rallies led by the Martin/Fulton family, the Reverends Al Sharpton and Jesse Jackson, Congresswoman Corrine Brown, and the NAACP. The Congresswoman from Miami/Dade County, Frederica Wilson, said many outlandish things. You may recall she is the one that wore the huge hats. Astounded by the racial tensions these protests produced, I prayed they would soon cease. Then, on Friday, March 23rd, we learned the leaders of the New Black Panther organization announced they had raised $10,000 in bounty for the capture of George Zimmerman "dead or alive," and I literally shook with fear. I didn't believe my ears.

Do we really live in a society where a group of people can go on national television and admit they have a bounty on another human being's head, yet no one is brought to justice for such a threat? I had to explain to our daughter that not all people are good, and even adults do bad things. She asked me directly, "Is "Georgie going to be killed or arrested?"

I struggled to find the words to allay her fear that someone she adores could be in such a terrible place. Tension in our home was at an all-time high as George felt attacked by dark and menacing forces. Every day, there was a possibility that it would be discovered that we were hiding George Zimmerman, the out-of-control neighborhood watch captain who killed an innocent teen making his way back home from the convenience store. I imagined people with guns coming to our door to take George away, or seeing him hurt before our eyes. Were we being watched? Would someone wait for us to leave and assault us with questions about George and his whereabouts? All of us felt the pressure of being prisoners in our own home during this time. But, we were adamant and committed to protecting our friends for as long as possible.

We have two dogs, and George and Shellie had one dog while staying with us. Their other dog was being kept by Shellie's father. It was necessary to take the dogs out for bathroom breaks and also for walks. Each time we left the house, we were constantly looking over our shoulders, hoping no one recognized it was George Zimmerman walking his dog in the neighborhood. As tensions over the case grew around the country, tension in our home rose, too. I knew George was becoming more and more depressed and very afraid.

Breanna, our ten-year-old daughter, had never been exposed to prejudice until the media brought it into our home. For the first time she was hearing words like "nigger" the "f-word" and "coon." (Later CNN admitted doctoring George's 911 tape to make the word "punk" sound like "coon.") She asked what these words meant as she was hearing them from the media and from friends at school; some who had attended Mr. Sharpton's rallies. I was shocked and angry that I would need to explain such words to her at such a young age.

I was troubled about the impact George's situation was having on Breanna. As spring break approached, her classmates were excited about the week off and all the fun they would have. Our Breanna, instead, was worried that her friend, George, would be either killed or arrested. Mark and I took Breanna away for a few days during the break and tried to reassure her that George was going to be fine and that he was safe. She was less fearful afterward, then she overheard the news about the $10,000 bounty raised by the new Black Panthers and she sensed the tension of the entire household. We tried to make sure she felt as safe as possible and reassured her again and again that we would all be okay, including George. There were many sleepless nights when I couldn't shake the real danger of harboring George and Shellie.

It seemed like the entire nation believed George Zimmerman was guilty of profiling, following, then murdering young Trayvon Martin. The only real truth at that time was that Trayvon Martin had been shot and killed in the gated community of The Retreat at Twin Lakes on February 26, 2012. The first reports were entirely skewed. George was first described as a 25-year-old white man; he is Hispanic and 28 years old. News reports stated he was a "self-appointed neighborhood watch captain." For the record, he had been asked to start a neighborhood watch program in the Twin Lakes community because it had been plagued with criminal activity in the months leading up to the shooting. George and Shellie had been victims of theft themselves and had witnessed other incidents in the neighborhood.

There were at least eight burglaries reported at Twin Lakes over the previous 14 months, several of them involving young black men. Only three weeks before George had the encounter with Trayvon, one of George's neighbors came home to find a burglar had broken into her home through a kitchen window. Expensive jewelry and a laptop were missing. The police were called out. Two witnesses gave statements that they saw a "young black man standing near the home." One witness believed it was the same one who had stolen his bike earlier. Officers responded to a call the next day and questioned three black men and one white man on bikes just outside the entrance to Twin Lakes. One of the men was identified as the same one seen near the home that was burglarized. The stolen laptop was found in the man's backpack.

There were other incidences that concerned residents. In July of 2011 a Twin Lakes resident awakened to find her sliding glass door open. She had left keys to a rental car on her dining table. The keys were missing along with the car that had been parked just outside. Later, the car was found abandoned.

Perhaps the most disturbing incident was six months before the shooting, when someone knocked on the door of a Twin Lakes resident. The woman looked through the window and didn't recognize the man standing outside her door. Just as she was walking away, she heard someone else at her back door. Frightened, she called the police then grabbed her small son and ran to an upstairs bedroom. She locked the bedroom door just as the second man gained entrance into her home. She was terrified and her son began to cry when one of the men tried to open the door of the bedroom. Both men ran when the police arrived, but they got away with the woman's digital camera and laptop. "It was terrible. I'm sure he could hear me in there because my son was crying and I was crying. Who knows what would have happened if the police hadn't been there," the young mother said.

Officers finally arrested the young man who broke into the woman's home and stole the laptop, but he was released because of his age. The minor lived in the neighborhood. Police reports indicate both the juvenile and the other man who robbed the woman were black.

Still another burglary occurred in August, and then in September a townhome under construction was vandalized. Perpetrators stopped up a toilet then left the water running, flooding the home and causing expensive damage. "There was a definite sense of fear," one neighbor said. Another commented how crime in the Twin Lakes area had residents "feeling afraid and scared."

During the days and nights that George and Shellie were in our home, I thought of all these things as fear permeated our household. Every day seemed to bring some new kind of speculation; the story would be twisted again and again, talking heads were dissecting the case, playing the 911 calls, and experts where chiming in with their opinion as to why Trayvon Martin had died. We tried to ease the pain for our friends as much as possible, but there was no escaping the mounting, overwhelming public clamor for George to be arrested.

I was not at the gated community of the night of February 26th and neither were the thousands, maybe millions, of people who feel they know *exactly* what happened. I have heard the rants from those who say they have been racially profiled themselves or know someone who has had similar experiences. I get that and it's wrong, but George Zimmerman is not that kind of racist villain. He is the kindest, most sincere, easygoing, non- judgmental person I have ever met.

I believe that Trayvon Martin did not have to die on the night of February 26th. Our friend, George Zimmerman cried loudly again and again for help. Many people heard the cries and called 911, but no one came to George's aid, no one intervened to break up the fight or even flicked on a porch light to interrupt the scuffle. The presence of others could have stopped the unfortunate chain of events, but we will never truly know. I have deep sympathy for the parents of young Trayvon Martin. Regardless of whether he had disciplinary issues, was suspended from school, even experimenting with drugs, it is tragic whenever or however a young person passes away.

However, I also feel deeply that George Zimmerman has been offered up as the sacrificial lamb for those who want to spew messages of hate and racism. As we were holed up in our home with the Zimmermans I prayed continuously, asking God to protect us. I also pleaded with Him to somehow give George some peace amid all the chaos and that he would soon be totally vindicated. As the hours turned to days and days into weeks, an ominous cloud hung over our household. I would say, other than the traumatic days just after the shooting, the darkest day was Friday, March 23rd, when he heard about the price on his head. He could not believe he was hated that much by so many. He was truly frightened for himself, his wife, and afraid for us, the family that was hiding him.

# Chapter 4

Our Family's New Normal

*Sondra*

Our new normal during the weeks of hiding George and Shellie Zimmerman were anything but. However, for our young daughter's sake, we tried to relieve the stress as much as possible. As stated, we were continually on guard anytime we left our home for any reason. But inside our home, we talked, played games, watched television and movies, and of course, monitored news reports to hear the latest developments or the most recent rumors regarding the case. I would glance over to measure George's response to the news coverage and see the look of confusion on his face. Sometimes he'd look away and stare as if deep in thought; other times there were tears in his eyes.

Mark constantly reassured George and Shellie that the police did not have enough evidence to arrest him, but the enormous pressure being placed on the police to make the arrest was mounting every day. Deep down, I think we all realized it was only a matter of time. However, my eternal optimist of a husband kept telling the couple again and again, "You can't panic until I do."

Trayvon's funeral on March 3rd was attended by elected officials around the state, teachers, classmates, and black leaders from across the country. Marches were organized and taking place everywhere it seemed, including the "Million Hoodie Marches," named after the "Million Man March" in the 1990's. The marches were being attended by thousands. George was more hurt than angry about the negative reactions across the country. The Trayvon Martin shooting was even big news overseas. None of us could get over the exaggerations being reported by the press and the widespread rush to judgment. George would ask often, "Why? Why are they being so mean?"

## Mark

George's mug shot was everywhere. The shooting was the lead story on every news report during those days of hiding. George would have been easily recognized if we had allowed him to go anywhere in public, so our routine was simple. He could not venture out of the house, or make contact with anyone but family and the police. He was still obligated to phone the police station and check in every day.

I know he was stir crazy and at times wanted to hold a press conference of his own and try to set the record straight in so many instances, but we convinced him to remain hidden and quiet. I knew if he spoke out or made any kind of statement in his own defense, the press would swallow him up and every word would be analyzed ad nauseam for days, even used against him. So, it followed that even his unavailability to the press and his silence was ridiculed as weakness and cowardice. He just couldn't get a break.

I was pleased with our attempts to keep George hidden while every news and media outlet in the country was trying to find him. Hollywood celebrities, political figures, and individuals with money are sought out and eventually discovered by the press, but here we were, "hiding in plain sight." It became sort of a local joke to refer to someone trying to evade or side step anything as, "pulling a George Zimmerman," or, if someone was unavailable or hard to locate, they were said to be "hidden like George Zimmerman."

Once, about two weeks after the shooting, at the peak of the madness, George and I ventured out during daylight hours to retrieve some clothing, documents and personal items from their home at Twin Lakes. It was a near disaster. I thought it would be relatively simple, easy in and easy out. I tried to plan every move like a battlefield tactician. I first proposed making the trip at 2 or 3 a.m. We could quietly arrive, park in their garage, close the garage door, load the items at our leisure, then head back undetected. George explained one giant problem with this plan: their garage door made more noise than a jingling Santa falling down a flight of stairs. "The neighbors on both sides would hear the door and come out to investigate," George said.

The press had already identified the address of the now famous George Zimmerman, so, his fear was that even well-intentioned neighbors might alert the media, even the police. Plan A was scrapped. Plan B, George's plan, was to make our way over before noon, perhaps 10:30 a.m., when most residents would be at work and the daytime noises would mask the rattling sound of the garage door opening. So, I drove my car over, while George sat in the passenger seat wearing oversized sunglasses and a baseball cap. At stoplights he would cover his face with the cap or scrunch down low in the seat.

As we were entering the gate at The Retreat at Twin Lakes, I was hoping the media interest would be elsewhere and we could get the items George needed quickly and easily. We were just yards away from his townhome when George instinctively pushed the garage door opener as he had done countless times before. I couldn't get the word, "Don't," out of my mouth in time.

The obscenely noisy garage door was nearly halfway up when I thought, *Darn, we should have done a "drive by" first, just to make sure no one was watching the residence.* It was too late. Just as the rattling garage door closed behind us and George disabled the house alarm inside, we heard rapid, forceful knocking at the front door. We knew it wasn't the Girl Scouts; those shifty media people had been watching. We both dove for cover, like soldiers avoiding artillery fire. As the knocking continued, we froze in our positions. George threw out some hand gestures I surprisingly understood right away. He warned me not to walk in front of the door because if anyone peered through the peep hole they would see our movements due to the sunlight streaming through the sliding glass doors toward the back of the home. I shrugged as if to say, *they already know where we are.*

The home was eerily quiet. On the February evening they left their place to stay with us, George and Shellie had turned off the heat and air conditioning unit so there was absolutely no sounds coming from inside. We listened to the conversation taking place at the front door. I assumed the speakers were a reporter and cameraman perhaps from a local newspaper.

"Are you sure it was George's residence you saw the car drive into?"

The other answered, "I think. I just can't be sure."

"What kind of car was it? Was it George's car?"

"I'm not sure. I was reading the paper."

"Well, this sure would be sweet if it was him," one offered.

"Yeah, I know," the other responded.

"Try to get another glance through the rear doors and see if anything's changed."

"Got it."

By the time the presumed cameraman made it to the rear doors of the townhome, George and I were halfway up the staircase, trying to tread lightly on the creaky stairs.

The siege had begun. We were trapped inside, and I could only imagine the lengths the reporter would go to in order to get a story. I saw that the man at the front door, whom I took as a journalist, was making a phone call.

Four minutes later, my cell phone vibrated in my pocket. Thank God, I had it set on vibrate mode. It was Sondra and Shellie calling from our home to say a local news station had announced during the noon broadcast they had located George Zimmerman and expected an exclusive interview with him later that day. They were confused by the announcement, so I filled them in on what was taking place.

Just then, we had a stroke of luck when George's neighbor pulled into his own driveway. The neighbor usually made it home for lunch, and he was arriving just as the second man returned to George's front door from the back of the house.

"Are you here to report on anything new?" the neighbor asked. He did not seem surprised with the media's presence, but sensed something was different about these two; they were like jittery hunting dogs that just chased a rabbit into a hole. They responded honestly.

"We were parked just up the street there watching George's home, hoping to get an exclusive interview. Have you seen George or Shellie? Do you know if they have made any visits to the house?"

"No, they haven't been back since that night (referring to the night of the shooting). My wife doesn't work and she'd know for sure if they had come back," the neighbor answered.

"Is she home right now? Did she hear someone enter through the garage about 15 minutes ago?"

George's neighbor called to his wife who soon appeared. He asked if she had heard anyone next door at George and Shellie's place.

"No, I've been here all morning, and I didn't hear anything."

He specifically asked again, "You didn't hear any noise or anything about 15 minutes ago?"

"No," she quickly replied.

The neighbor seemed 100% sure his wife, "who stayed up on the neighborhood news and knew the comings and goings of just about everyone," would have heard if anyone had opened the Zimmerman's garage. George later admitted being most nervous about the neighbor's answer as to whether she had heard us entering the home. If she had answered, "Yes," the gig was up. The reporter would have simply waited us out.

As it was, the guys intent on an interview, were not quite ready to give up. They parked their car on the street directly in front of the Zimmermans' driveway, effectively blocking our way should we try to leave.

We were listening to the exchange between the neighbors and the news men from an upstairs bedroom while peeking out from tiny cracks in the curtains. The reporter, wearing a nice shirt and tie, made another call on his phone while the sloppily dressed cameraman affixed his bulky camera onto a tripod which he set in front of the house. Suddenly, the reporter finished his call and turned to look directly at the second-story window where George stood, looking out. Then the cameraman points to the window and aims the camera in our direction.

*Oh, no,* I thought. I had failed to warn George of something I learned from Warrants Deputies years before. When seeking a subject, they would often watch the curtains of a residence closely to see if they moved even slightly. Curtains move at the tiniest motion, even in response to someone's breathing.

Many times the guys in our Warrants Unit would give us road patrol deputies a handful of papers with a fugitive's name on each. During "down times" we would try and track these people down. I would say 99% of the time we would come across the subjects by accident and happen to have the warrant form in hand to make an arrest. The Warrants Deputies were much more experienced and seemed to personify the phrase, "Work smarter, not harder." In no way did I mind helping them to nab their fugitives, because I learned so much from these super cool, calm warrants guys. Checking to see if curtains were moving was one of those lessons.

Realizing the two men below were looking upstairs, I couldn't walk quickly over to George's window from mine without causing the curtain to move, so I was the one who sent George a hand signal of my own: *Be still and don't move the curtain.*

Not only was it quiet inside the home, it was quiet outside, too; not so much of a breeze stirring. We could hear the two men's footsteps clearly and hear every word of their conversation. Finally, their disappointed sighs let us know they would soon be going. Like fishermen who had had a bad fishing day, body language told us they were giving up.

They had the advantage, but didn't know it. We could keep quiet for hours, but wouldn't be able to get out of the garage until they left. I suppose we could have crept out the back door and walked back to our home close by, but that would mean leaving my car in the garage, leaving the home alarm off and the sliding glass doors would be unlocked. That was out of the question for George.

So, we discussed having to be trapped there for hours, even days. We snickered at that possibility, and then caught the final break. The dejected news team, after two hours of surveillance, decided to "load the car and reset."

We felt like outlaws planning a jail break. If the newsmen were merely going to back their car up four or five parking spaces and continue to wait while parked along the road, then George and I envisioned pulling the car out, then being involved in a low speed chase through the neighborhood, both parties obeying speed signs and road signals. We would then have to make sure to ditch the reporters so they couldn't follow us back to my home.

In the next few seconds I thought of a way to keep the non-dramatic chase from occurring. I called a friend, RJ, who owns a truck. RJ is a former Desert Storm Marine, and the epitome of the brave men and women who protect and honor our great country with their military service. After I gave him my location, in low tones, I asked, "RJ, could you drive your truck over and park sideways, in order to block a road nearby? If you could prevent a car from following me after I go through an intersection, it would be greatly appreciated."

His only response was, "Sure, but how do I deal with the people after I block their way?"

I told him they were harmless, but he just needed to keep them from following me. To which he said, "No problem." RJ is such a calm, cool guy that he has never asked, to this day, what the circumstances were behind my request for help. To me, that is a mark of true friendship, trust and loyalty.

Turns out, we didn't need RJ and his truck, after all. The vehicle with the news crew pulled forward around the more than quarter of a mile circle road inside the complex coming to rest several residences away facing George's apartment. This is perhaps where they were originally parked.

The Twin Lakes sub division is laid out in a circle. For a visitor coming in the front entrance, they would travel around toward the back to find George and Shellie's townhome. I can't say for sure where the news team ended up because we scurried out while that loudspeaker of a garage door was opening. As it closed behind us we simply followed them out and then left the scene going in the same direction, but, at a safe distance. We then took a side exit toward the back of the complex. They never saw us. The cat did not see the mouse slip away. Whew!

I made a quick follow-up call to RJ to inform him I got away from my pursuers. His response was a personal compliment to me: "I had no doubt." Then it was back to our house where the girls were anxious to hear about the encounter. George and I licked our mental wounds and did a reset of our own.

George often referred to how calm I was under pressure. I suppose I don't give it much thought as it is just who I am. I had learned from the best, and it was second nature to me to control my emotions during times of fear, anxiety, or chaos. George seemed eager to learn this character trait and I hope it serves him well for the rest of his life. I told George, "Remove panic from your toolbox and a whole laundry list of adverse outcomes seems to vanish."

George listened intently whenever I talked about remaining calm by mentally slowing down your thought process to grasp that elusive quality called, "clarity." The best way to have clarity in a dangerous situation is to try to simulate it often. Play it over in your head, asking, "What would I do if …?"

Even when we were practicing at the gun range I would suggest scenarios to George that might require bulls-eye marksmanship in tension-filled moments. Clarity doesn't arrive the day you graduate from the police academy. Rookies often embody the descriptive phrase, "more courage than brains." They may rush into hot situations without the experience to resolve it efficiently. True clarity of a situation can be better experienced at a distance than when you are thrust into the middle of the dust storm.

If you study how great detectives collect information (evidence) at a crime scene, you'll notice their calm, methodical pace. Street cops need to own that same calm when arriving on a scene, even before they exit their vehicle. When I shared such tactics with George he seemed fascinated by the resolve necessary to stay calm under pressure.

George absorbed every tidbit of information my experience in law enforcement and the military had taught me. On one occasion George asked if I thought he had what it took to be a police officer. I paused for a moment then replied, "To be any kind of cop you should be as numb as a post to the insults hurled at you daily, dumb enough to rush toward the trouble many are running away from, and be willing to sacrifice everything for your fellow officers and even total strangers, regardless of the cost. In these regards, George, I find your qualifications impeccable. Plus, you have a genuine humility and a willingness to learn that gives you an advantage over other young cops who think they know it all."

I told him some officers are loud and cocky because of their own insecurity; others are quiet, calm, and reserved because they are fully aware of their insecurities. I meant every word: I thought George had the makings of a great cop.

Talk about a humbling experience: mine came when I was about seventeen years old. My father and I were sitting in the den watching a John Wayne movie on television. We had earlier taken a few rifles and pistols to a local shooting range for practice. It was my job after target practice to clean the guns so I had spread a few old towels on the floor in front of the television along with the three rifles we had used at the range. Customarily I would run a cleaning brush down the barrel of each and use a toothbrush to remove any carbon spots. As I worked on the guns and watched the movie at the same time, I noticed my father had fallen asleep in his chair and was snoring loudly before the movie was half over.

I first checked the two monster caliber rifles, a .308 bolt action and a .3030 lever action rifle, to confirm they were unloaded and then I cleaned each, oiled them and set them aside. I took up the rapid fire .22 caliber plinking rifle, seemingly harmless, especially when compared to the other two with their ridiculous recoil, not realizing that this rifle concealed a secret.

The two big heavy hitting rifles were fired last at the range. Just before, we had fired the .22 caliber into the man-sized paper target, then reloaded it, planning to fire it later, but two boxes of 20 rounds for each big rifle had sapped us of energy. Remember, the big gun provides forty merciless hammer blows into your shoulder, as if delivered by Thor himself. The smaller .22 caliber (I'll call it the humiliator), like its counterparts, was unloaded at the range by rapidly snapping the chamber open, thus flinging the unfired rounds more than a meter away. Apparently this round flinging was so engrossing that when the bullets stopped ejecting from the chamber, I gave it five or six customary snaps to insure the firearm was not loaded, but overlooked the #1 rule my dad, a hard-ass retired Detroit cop, had drilled into me, "Look at the chamber and port with a stern eye to guarantee it's empty."

I was about to find out the cost of not checking the chamber. I was holding the rifle with the butt stock resting on the towel in the den with the barrel pointing straight up toward the ceiling. I conducted another five or six snaps of the bolt. Instead, if I had just looked in the chamber, I would've been slapped in the face because the ejector pin held the very last bullet in a death grip unwilling to release it until it committed some kind of mischief.

In my extremely lame defense, the movie we were watching was *The Green Berets*, and it was nearing the climactic ending when the firebase defended by the Americans was being overrun and an eruption of napalm engulfed the Vietnamese troops. At that precise moment on screen, I placed my index finger against the trigger to release the tension on the firing pin spring; not even looking at the rifle as I innocently squeezed the trigger.

A blast of expanding gas and smoke exploded from the end of the rifle! I heard Dad suck air in rapidly through clenched teeth. As if in slow motion, I jumped up and spun toward Dad, who was slowly opening his eyes. My grizzly tempered father was sitting as he always did in his chair, shirtless, shoeless, and sockless, wearing only cargo pocketed shorts, but it was clear where the bullet struck. A trickle of blood slowly made its way down Dad's chest from a small hole between his left nipple and his sternum.

I was in shock; I couldn't utter a sound. I stood there mouth open, waiting to react to any command given me, but Dad didn't say a word. He pulled the lever on his recliner that allowed him to stand. The grimace on his face from the bullet's impact was now replaced by a completely expressionless gaze. He deliberately, but unhurriedly, walked to the bathroom where he scratched a medium sized piece of flattened copper out of the wound on his chest. He reached for a cotton ball, then an oversized Band-Aid. The volume of blood coming from the wound had slowed to no more than what a nosebleed would cause. He observed the cotton ball bulging out of the side of Band-Aid and was convinced, I suppose, that he wouldn't be getting blood on Mom's carpet. Mom, a nurse, would have pursued that mystery all the way to a full confession.

Fortunately, Mom did not look toward the ceiling in the den over the next week. The pesky little .22 fired through a wooden paneled ceiling fan blade, then, flattened partially by the concrete ceiling, broke apart and sent a portion of the copper jacketed little devil into Dad's chest, a soft landing place. I followed Dad from the bathroom back to the TV room where he went straight to the television set, ran his hands over the screen checking for damage. He then muttered the only words spoken during the whole ordeal. He said, "Good, nothing went into the TV."

As he turned to take the few steps back to his chair, he flashed me a barely perceptible smile. I will never forget Dad's coolness in a moment that could have had disastrous results. I wanted to learn, and did learn from the incident that neither of us have spoken of since.

George received a lot of criticism for carrying a gun on the night of February 26, 2012, when he encountered young Trayvon Martin. Amid all the debate over "the right to carry" issues that ensued, there was also national debate about Florida's "stand your ground" law, which basically gives any citizen the right to use deadly force if they or others feel threatened or feel their life is in danger. There are those I realize who believe gun laws need to be rethought and refined. Their mantra is "Why do we love guns so much in this country? Aren't guns killing machines, designed to hurt or kill?" However, they overlook the many incidences in which guns are used to protect and defend. It is the Constitutional right of every citizen to bear arms.

George and I enjoyed the male camaraderie that target practice and knowledge of firearms provided, but I can also verify that George adhered to basic gun safety at all times. He never brandished a weapon, or even spoke of using it to instill fear, or to control another. However, even residents of Twin Lakes who supported George's effort to patrol the area did not think it was wise for him to take a gun along on the evening he noticed Trayvon Martin walking inside the gated community. On the other hand, one resident stated that Shellie implored her husband to get a gun for protection as well.

Citizen patrol groups are always cautioned to leave weapons at home; instead focus on observing and reporting potential crime. They specifically warn groups against trying to do the job of the police. I understand the philosophy behind the caution, but here's the thing. George Zimmerman's gun was legal; he had a legal license and also a license to conceal it.

Many have turned the shooting of Trayvon Martin into a debate on gun laws. Most are convinced the presence of

George's firearm resulted in the death of Trayvon. How can anyone say that? George felt he was going to be suffocated to death as Trayvon's hands covered his nose and mouth. Death by Trayvon's hands or George's gun; tragic any way you look at it.

As George waited inside our home, in hiding, these and other issues were daily fodder that only added to his stress. Three weeks after the shooting, George's father, Robert (Bob), found a local attorney, Craig Sonner, willing to represent him if needed. George had not signed any binding contract as yet, but one day the attorney asked if I could accompany him to George and Shellie's home at Twin Lakes for the purpose of getting a more recent photo of George. The only one released had been the non-flattering mug shot. We obtained a photo of George that depicted more accurately his present appearance. As soon as the attorney made it available, the press began to post the more recent photo, but George's mug shot had already made an all-important first impression in the minds of most Americans.

Toward the end of that same three-week period, that's when news broke that the Black Panther organization had set a bounty on George's head; $10,000 dead or alive. It was the straw that broke the camel's back. George was at his lowest point. He was fearful of course, but mostly for the safety of Shellie, and me and Sondra and Breanna. He wanted to leave our home as soon as possible and go out of state. I said, "No, George, you can't do this. I am prepared to handle any threat, even men with guns. I'm ready for them."

"I just can't deal with the added worry about the safety of all of you because of me. If something happened to any one of you, I could never forgive myself," George said.

To which I replied, "If you leave and get injured or harmed, I will never forgive myself."

George was adamant this time and on March 23rd, after a month in our home, he packed a few things and traveled to another undisclosed location, probably up north. He had relatives including brothers, sisters, and cousins who were willing to take him in for however long it would take for this thing to pass. He also believed there would be less press coverage and clamor away from the Orlando area.

Shellie stayed behind with us for the time being, and it was heartbreaking to see them saying their goodbyes, neither one knowing what would happen in the future or when they would be together again.

*Sondra*

Shellie's 25th birthday fell during the weeks of hiding. George invited her parents over to our home, and we had a small birthday party to celebrate. He gave me $200 to take Shellie out for a shopping trip, "so she could get away from everything."

Finally, it was apparent that George had made up his mind to separate himself from us and his wife for our own safety. He had become even more fearful over the numerous death threats, and just thought it was the best thing to do.

On the day he was loading up his truck to relocate somewhere out of state, suddenly our driveway was blocked by two vehicles with several black people in both cars. George came running wildly back into the house, shouting for Shellie to have her firearm ready should the people out front break through the front door. George himself climbed the stairs and was watching the group from a second story window. Our daughter, Breanna, home at the time, ran to her room and locked the door, terrified of what may occur. My sister and nephews were also visiting that day; we all stood frozen in place until I ventured to look out and see that I recognized the people in the vehicles. They were actually friends of a neighbor. I announced this news to George and everyone inside and we breathed a collected sigh of relief. For George it only affirmed he was making the right decision to move out of state for the safety of all.

George loaded a few belongings and his dog, Oso, into the truck and he and Shellie lingered awhile, saying goodbye before a final kiss. I'm sure the drive was freeing to George as he sped along the highways north to safety. In fact, he would later describe his trip as an escape, symbolic of freedom and normalcy once again. For a month he had felt trapped, hunted, and fearful. As he traveled, he felt freer with every mile. That freedom would be short-lived.

# Chapter Five

## Who Are We?

*Mark*

We thought we would let you know a little about us personally and perhaps offer more insight as to why we felt compelled to write this book in defense of our friends, George and Shellie Zimmerman.

So, who are we, other than friends of George Zimmerman, who remains one of the most hated men in America? I was born Mark Charles Osterman on May 27, 1968, in Detroit, Michigan. My mother and father divorced when I five years old. Both remarried, and I have one biological sister, three stepsisters and one stepbrother.

My mother and her husband live in Flint, Michigan, and my father and his wife now reside in New Smyrna Beach, Florida. The family moved from Detroit to Wadsworth, Ohio, when I was in the fourth grade. At eighteen I enlisted in the Army and completed infantry and airborne schools at Fort Benning, Georgia, then did a two-year tour in Germany, completing my first four years at Fort Stewart, Georgia.

After the service I moved to Florida, far away from the cold Michigan winters, where I pursued a career in law enforcement and spent time enjoying my passion for scuba diving. I have earned ten diving certifications to date. I have always followed college football and been an avid fan of recreational pistol shooting.

You may recall that Sadaam Hussein decided to invade Kuwait in August of 1990, and by that December I was recalled to active duty to form an infantry brigade during Operation Desert Shield/Storm. I was first sent back to Germany to act as a strategic reserve. Soon after, the "mother of all battles" proved successful. So, "shock and awe" saw to it that we weren't needed, and it was back to civilian life for me. I returned to Florida and was employed by the Seminole County Sheriff's Department as a Deputy Sheriff. I'm currently a law enforcement officer with the Department of Homeland Security.

I cherish my roles as husband and father. My friendships are also important to me and consider friends as family. This is why I was brokenhearted for my friend, George Zimmerman, on the evening of the shooting of Trayvon Martin. I remained concerned and prayerful for George and Shellie. I just wanted him to be treated fairly. This entire situation was overlaid with politics, innuendo and half truths from the start, but I kept trying to reassure George he could not possibly be arrested and therefore would not need to stand trial. I truly believed there was no evidence to support an arrest. I still do.

*Sondra*

I am a native Floridian, born on September 30, 1974, in Orlando. My parents also divorced, and my mother and stepfather live in DeBary, Florida, while my dad and his wife live in DeLand, Florida. I have one sister, a brother, and two stepsisters. From the time I graduated high school I have worked in the mortgage/finance industry for various companies and brokers.

While working in the collections department for one of those companies, I telephoned a Mark Osterman who was listed as a reference for a client who was behind on payments owed our firm. My purpose was to obtain additional contact information for locating the client. Mark was not only helpful with information, he promised to personally drive the client to my office within the week when he was off duty, and he did just that. When he and the client arrived, my co-workers and I thought Mark was very handsome in his deputy sheriff's uniform. From then on, whenever I needed help contacting this client, I would contact Mark. After a month or two, we went on our first date and were engaged after five months, then married nine months later on November 2, 1996.

After moving into our first home in 1998, we began trying to have a baby, but became discouraged again and again. After several medical procedures and hormone treatments, we finally were pregnant and elated. On July 18, 2001, our precious baby girl, Breanna Merri, was born. Due to the medical issues, Breanna would be our only child, but we were a happy family of three. Now eleven years old, Breanna will be in the sixth grade this year. She enjoys scrapbooking, swimming, loves playing soccer, tennis, baseball and basketball, and is a black belt in Tae Kwon Do. She has brought us so much joy.

Our personal lives and family principles are deeply rooted in the Christian faith. Mark attended a Lutheran church as a youngster, and I grew up in a spirited Pentecostal church. We were married in a Methodist church and now our family worships together at a non-denominational church not far from our home.

I can't pinpoint one specific reason as to why we were drawn to George and Shellie Zimmerman. They were caring, loving, genuine people, easy to be around, warm, and embracing. We would never have dreamed that our friendship would be tested to the extreme when George was accused of profiling then murdering young Trayvon Martin last February. We miss the Zimmermans. We miss the conversations, the fun, the time spent just hanging out together with our friends, one of whom will be on trial soon for second degree murder. It seems as if it all has been the worst nightmare and we will all wake up to find it didn't happen at all.

George faces a possible lengthy prison sentence if found guilty. We hope not, we pray not, but many people feel this is the least punishment for the gun-toting, over-zealous neighborhood watch captain who took the life of an unarmed teenager. Of course, we believe otherwise.

### Breanna Osterman (10 years old)

I met George at my mom's office, and he was so funny and nice to me. He told me jokes and sometimes he let me help him with his work. Once, George and Shellie took me to Aquatica, and we had a lot of fun. George rode the rides with me, then he also let me go on some rides by myself. That was a fun day! We also went to Disney World together a couple of times and that was fun, too. Around Christmas time, we all went to see the Osborne lights at Disney (me, George and Shellie and Mom and Dad). I had hurt my leg and couldn't walk around so we got a wheelchair and George pushed me around the whole time, until it was time to leave. One time, he gave me a job; walking his dog, Oso. He paid me $15 and that was really nice. George is the nicest guy I have ever met and really funny. I think what is happening to him right now is not fair and it scares me. I hope he's all right and doesn't get hurt or go to jail. I love George very much and miss him. I hope I can see him soon.

*Sondra*

Three years ago when Breanna was about seven years old, she wondered why she could never hear Santa when he came to drop off her gifts. "If I could hear him or his reindeer, then I could let my friends know he is real," she said with a little girl's reasoning. George overheard us talking about this and decided he would dress as Santa that Christmas, place gifts under the tree, making just enough noise in doing so that Breanna would hear him as he did his Santa magic.

That Christmas Eve our family read the Christmas story from the Bible, as is our tradition, then we heard something (or someone) in the living room. Mark asked Breanna and me to stay put while he checked it out. Then, he returned, telling Breanna to be extra quiet as he directed her to walk on tiptoe, then peek around the door. You should have seen her face. There was Santa (George) hard at work placing gifts around the tree. She ran to her bed and begged us to go to bed quickly, so Santa wouldn't take away her gifts.

The next day, Christmas Day, Breanna was telling all her cousins that she had seen "Santa's butt" while he put presents under our tree. Later, during a party at Shellie's parents' home, she was telling George what she had seen the night before. He listened intently and acted as if he was fascinated by her story. Breanna remembers that special Christmas to this day and still has no clue that Santa was actually her friend, George; the George we know and love.

## Mark

As Shellie continued living with us following George's departure in April, the media coverage became even more biased and brutal. Other militant blacks around the country joined the new Black Panther group in denigrating

George's character, demanding he be arrested. Even politicians wore hoodies to work. One representative, speaking from the floor of the Senate, stood demanding justice for Trayvon, and continued irreverently as the chairman's gavel tried to silence his antics.

In my six years as a Deputy Sheriff in Seminole County I saw and experienced things the average person would never see, not even on the reality television shows featuring real cops. No Hollywood writer could conceive the craziness and bizarre people policemen and fire rescue personnel have to deal with on a daily basis.

I've responded to residences for every reason imaginable, like showing up to explain custody paperwork served by court order, or arriving to negotiate peace between neighbors because overlapping sprinklers are making one resident's grass grow differently than the others. I once entered a residence where a six-foot Nazi flag was exhibited and Hitler's portrait hung over the fireplace mantel. Of course, I never indicated how offensive this display was to me, a product of a German Catholic mother and father with English-Jewish heritage. Ancestors from both sides of my family bravely made the journey to America to embrace all she stands for. But you see it all the time in law enforcement; minds distorted and poisoned by prejudice and hate. Even when presented with absolute truth, such people, like those above, have been programmed for racial divide, which brings to mind George's situation.

Similar to the skinheads and Neo Nazi groups most civil folks abhor, another group, just as racially prejudiced, the new Black Panthers, passed judgment on George; a man who at that point had made no public comment, no evidence had been presented, and no arrest had been made. The case was being investigated. It seems to me that before an individual or group leaps to conclusions, they would *want* to back up their opinions with facts; they would *want* to wait to hear all angles of a topic. Even a self-serving media eager for higher ratings wouldn't report innuendos to stir more outrage in this case – would they? They did.

I was a huge fan of the consummate professional newsman, the late Walter Cronkite. His reports were always straightforward, well thought out, unbiased, and devoid of hype. I couldn't help but wonder how Mr. Cronkite would have reported on the investigation into Trayvon Martin's death. I respect Sean Hannity and his approach to reporting. When I caught his show, I appreciated his insistence for cooler heads to prevail regarding this case; he called for evidence first, then opinions and discussions afterward.

George and Shellie kept in contact regularly while they were separated. They would call each other or Skype every day. I'm sure it made the time apart a little easier. But the pressure was mounting every day; loud voices were calling for an arrest to be made. The Zimmermans lived from moment to moment, just waiting for the other shoe to fall. They wouldn't have to wait much longer.

# Chapter Six

## Headlines:
## Zimmerman Arrested and Jailed!

*Mark*

As mentioned, from the onset of the incident that occurred between my best friend, George Zimmerman and Trayvon Martin, George had not contractually committed to be represented by a specific attorney. George's father, Robert (called Bob), without George's permission, had contacted attorney Craig Sonner and even given Sonner permission to speak on George's behalf, but George himself had major reservations. A contract from Sonner was sent (actually faxed) up north where George was staying after he left our home in April. When George told Sonner he wanted a friend of his father to look it over before signing, Sonner pressured him, "We don't have time for that, George. You need to sign it, get it notarized and returned to me as soon as possible. Trust me."

"No, this is important, I need to slow down and look at the contract seriously before we proceed," George replied, much to Sonner's chagrin.

George sent me a copy of the contract. After reading it, my first impression was that it seemed way "over the top," in regard to the money Sonner would make from the case; it guaranteed a huge upfront percentage of any profits gained from future book deals, movie opportunities, television appearances, articles, whether Sonner remained George's attorney or not. I just didn't have a good feeling about the whole thing and relayed my thoughts to George. "I just don't like the verbiage in the contract at all. It seems inordinately slanted toward the attorney making money, instead of representing you fairly."

George had already made up his mind, but appreciated my input. He never had a good feeling about Sonner either and just didn't trust him fully, so the contract was never signed or returned.

After realizing they had lost the opportunity to represent George, you may recall Sonner and another partner, announced to the media they were not going to represent

George because he was "not revealing his whereabouts to them, going against their counsel and speaking to the police directly." They made it sound like it was *their* decision to drop George when it was George who decided against using their firm. It seemed as though every story having anything to do with George was slanted negatively, spun, to make George seem indecisive, weak, a gun-toting out-of-control vigilante.

One of the questions discussed on various talk shows was how someone like George Zimmerman, who had a prior arrest for violent behavior, was issued a gun permit. I mentioned previously George's arrest when he was just 21 years old for battery on a law enforcement officer and obstructing justice. Evidently, before that case was even resolved, George had some "love" problems in 2007. A domestic abuse report was filed by his ex-fiancée, a hairdresser. She also requested a restraining order against him because he was "trolling her neighborhood checking on her." Evidently a pushing match between the two started when George went to retrieve some personal items from her place. In response, George asked for a restraining order against her, because she slapped, choked and clawed him on that occasion. They were both ordered to stay away from each other and no charges were ever filed. George called police again in October to report his tires were slashed on his Dodge Durango. He suspected an ex-boyfriend of the girlfriend, but the guy denied responsibility, then threatened to file another restraining order against George for "annoying" him with text messages.

My take on all of this is that George was growing up during this time. All of us have sewn wild oats, made stupid decisions, exhibited some rebellion in our younger days; things we certainly would not want to be made public. During that same year, 2007, George married Shellie Nicole Dean and, in my opinion, became a different man. I am sure Shellie's love and expectations of George caused him to focus on lifestyle changes, priorities, and his future family. I hope in some small ways, too, our friendship with George and Shellie provided him with good examples to observe and respect.

*Sondra*

After George relocated out of state, Shellie continued attending nursing school, fulfilling a promise she'd made to George. He didn't want all the "madness" extenuating from the Trayvon Martin shooting to keep her from graduating. Things in our home were still extremely stressful, but George and Shellie were able to communicate every day, and this helped to ease Shellie's concerns a great deal.

She was especially elated to hear that George would be returning for a visit on April 11th, and they made plans. George would pick Shellie up, and then the couple would travel up north to spend a long weekend together.

That same day, April 11th, as George was preparing for his trip to Florida, I happened to be watching television and heard that Angela Corey, the state's prosecuting attorney, would be conducting a press conference to announce an arrest warrant had been issued for George. The moment had come that we hoped and prayed and thought, perhaps naively, would never come.

I hurriedly sent a text to Shellie, who was doing her clinical work at a nearby hospital, and informed her of the announcement. She immediately then called George on his cell phone and nervously reported the news that he was now a wanted man. George was incredulous. He didn't know what to do next, so on his way down toward Florida, he phoned his contact within the Florida Department of Law Enforcement. At this time he was about 123 miles from Sanford near Jacksonville. After learning George's whereabouts, the officer told him he would have an officer meet him at a particular mile marker. The officer would then escort George to the Jacksonville Police Department where he would surrender to the authorities.

I'm certain that George must have felt blindsided, especially after we had been telling him for weeks there was no chance he would be arrested. We just couldn't see how any evidence could be produced to warrant charges. To this day we believe this is a clear-cut case of simple self defense. But, public outcry had won; now, it was a new game, and those who had clamored for George to be arrested would not be satisfied just with his arrest; they wanted blood.

*Mark*

While driving to meet the officer who would lead him to the Jacksonville Police Department, George called Mark O'Mara, a well known and respected Florida attorney to ask if Mr. O'Mara would represent him. O'Mara agreed and immediately began to give George direction as to what he should and should not do during the next few hours. Turns out that I knew O'Mara from serving as a deputy for Seminole County and he remembered me when we saw each other later. O'Mara came highly recommended and in fact had a successful track record for representing fellow attorneys when needed.

It was breaking news across the country! George Zimmerman would face charges for shooting Trayvon Martin! We were in shock. Forty-five days after the incident at The Retreat at Twin Lakes, prosecutor Angela Corey was appointed by the Governor to head up the investigation and the case against George. Corey is up for re-election and taking the lead in such a high-profile case had to guarantee her lots of press coverage in the coming months. The charge was second degree murder. Here's a portion of the comments Corey made during her lengthy press conference on April 11th:

*"Today, we charged George Zimmerman with second degree murder. The team with me has worked tirelessly to find answers to Trayvon Martin's death."*

*"We prosecute on facts and we will continue to seek the truth."*

*"Mr. Zimmerman is indeed in custody and I will not tell you where."*

(Gheez, lady – get a clue. Before the conference was over people knew where Zimmerman was being held.)

*"We do not discuss the information involved in a case."*

*"Mr. Zimmerman turned himself in and was subsequently arrested on the capias that was issued."*

(Lawyers! What in the heck does "capias" mean?)

Following was the prosecutor's response to the question as to why it took a total of forty-five days before an arrest was made:

*"I can tell you that the investigation was in full mode and that the governor appointed us less than three weeks ago, and we had to make sure we had everything proper in place in order to prosecute. We have many homicides in Florida and it takes us time to investigate them all."*

*Ben Crump, the attorney for Trayvon Martin's family, reported they were very pleased to hear the announcement of Zimmerman's arrest and that charges were filed.*

A second degree murder charge in Florida is ordinarily charged when there is a fight or some altercation that results in death and where there is no premeditated plan to kill someone. I can only imagine the fall-out if George hadn't been charged with something! It was clear to me that a mob of people who know very little of how our system *should* work finally "got their way." The people who were clamoring, "No Justice, No Peace," bullied the authorities with threats to riot if an arrest was not made. The threat was real. Imagine the billions of dollars of damage in every city in America if an arrest had not been made. All this is at George Zimmerman's expense. And what if the verdict isn't to their liking? The voices are not going to stop or be satisfied with only an arrest and trial; they want the only acceptable verdict ... guilty as charged!

## Sondra

We could not believe this was happening. Listening to Angela Corey's meandering press conference about the charges against George was like taking a blow to the stomach. George was able to contact Shellie on his drive down from Jacksonville to Sanford. Even during this time, he was more concerned with how Shellie and the rest of the family were doing than for himself. He was very disheartened to be under arrest for defending himself, and he told Shellie he was "more uncertain of his future than ever before." Of course, Shellie was concerned about his safety, due to the death threats and the volatility of the Trayvon Martin camp. He assured her he was safe. Two unmarked police vehicles followed him from behind, and he could hear a helicopter just overhead.

Upon arrival at the Sanford Police Department, he was immediately booked and jailed. Jailed! All along we had told George this couldn't happen; we probably lost some credibility in George and Shellie's eyes. I can tell you that from this point on, they were not as open with information and personal thoughts and plans as before. Where Mark was once George's only "go to" person for everything, now attorneys, family members, and others were guiding him through this time. However, we hoped George knew how much we still cared for him and Shellie and how we earnestly prayed for them as the story continued to develop.

Of course, we understand that it was important that we not have contact with George during this time, due to the fact that we could be called as witnesses. George's attorney advised him, I'm sure, that information could not be passed between us any longer. And, indeed, the limited contact became a way of protecting the Zimmermans and us.

After turning himself in, George appeared in court the next day to hear the charges against him and for an arraignment date to be set. George did not enter a plea at that time and no bail was set as yet. George's attorney, Mark O'Mara, requested a bond hearing soon. Within fifteen days, prosecutors would start providing the defense with witness statements, police reports, photos, and discovery evidence that could be used against him. Like the circus it was, people all over the country knew about the evidence because it was released to the public almost immediately, and the media began to dissect the information again and again. At his very first court appearance, George apologized to the Martin family. He has remained extremely sorry that the altercation ended so tragically.

Shellie would fill us in as to George's state of mind while in jail, but Mark and I never spoke to him directly during this time. We asked Shellie to convey to George that we loved him and were thinking of him. He would often break down during their conversations, "I can't believe everything you are going through. I am so sorry this has to affect you."

Shellie later told us, because they knew jail house calls were recorded, they referred to Mark as "safety" and they called me "safety's wife" when speaking about us.

Just after George's arrest, his sister from up north came to Florida and stayed in our home along with Shellie. She was the sweetest person. George also has another sister who lives here in Florida. A meeting was scheduled with Mark O'Mara, George's new attorney, to determine the next step in securing George's release. A group of us met on Saturday, April 14th, at a hotel in Lake Mary. Along with O'Mara, Shellie and her father, Mark and I, George's parents, and the visiting sister were present for the meeting while George's brother was on Skype during the meeting Breanna came along also, but sat in another room. Afterward, we had a better idea of what we needed to do to help George to gain not only immediate freedom but also, hopefully, his complete freedom.

## Mark

George's father, Robert Zimmerman, whom the family calls Bob, along with his brother, Robert, appeared on Sean Hannity's program on Fox News. His father reported that George told him a few more details about the scuffle between George and Trayvon Martin on the rainy night of February 26th.

"George told me that he tried to squirm onto the grass from the sidewalk, when the gun he wore in a holster at his waist was exposed. According to George, the young man saw the gun and said something like, 'you're going to die tonight' or 'you're going to die now." Bob Zimmerman also confirmed the voice calling for help on the 911 recordings was his son's voice.

The brother, Robert, also commented during the interview that George had told him Trayvon saw the gun during the struggle and tried to take it, saying, "You die tonight!" Both were convinced George was in a struggle for his life and fired the gun only in self defense.

Nine days after his arrest on April 20th, George's bail hearing was conducted. Witnesses for his defense, which included George's family, would be questioned at our home over the next few days. Interviews with each were conducted by phone for security reasons. A notary arrived to swear in each witness, and their testimony was recorded. Of course none of us were allowed to watch the actual bail hearing itself, prior to our testimony being taken, but we recorded George's hearing to view later.

We were extremely encouraged by the outcome of the bail bond hearing. George would be released once bail was posted. The presiding judge set bond at $150,000, which meant the family had to come up with $15,000. It could have been so much worse. We took the low amount of bail as a sign that the judge thought the case was not solid and saw George as a low flight risk. We were all very hopeful at this point.

On the morning of April 23$^{rd}$, Shellie secured a rental car and arrived around midnight that night to pick up George from the John E. Polk Correctional Facility. Mark had secured a couple of bulletproof vests and encouraged them to wear the vests until they were safely out of town. Shellie told us George seemed subdued on the day of his release, but extremely relieved to be out of jail and with Shellie. They both vanished that night and went into hiding at another undisclosed location. We have not seen the couple since.

*Mark*

I knew it was probably just a matter of time before someone in law enforcement would want to talk to me about my relationship with George. As mentioned, I was recognized and greeted by other Sanford police officers whenever I accompanied George to the station. Soon after the Florida Department of Law Enforcement took over the investigation of the Trayvon Martin shooting, someone informed them that I was somehow involved or connected to George. Not long after his arrest they approached me and asked if I would be willing to come in for a completely "voluntary" discussion which would not even be taped. I'm sure they were hoping I would be able to supply information that would help with a criminal or civil rights conviction case.

I arrived at the Orlando Federal Building and was escorted to a spacious room and seated with my back to the door, further affirming that I would be free to leave at any time. I would be questioned by an F.B.I. agent and an agent with the Florida Department of Law Enforcement (FDLE). They reiterated that the session was completely voluntary. I agreed and the interview was underway.

They first asked about the night of February 26th and the events that transpired after I was informed of the shooting at The Retreat at Twin Lakes. One F.B.I. agent informed me that this report would be seen at the "highest levels" and gave me a rather emotionless stare, possibly to get a "free response" from me without having to ask a question. When I didn't bite on that or respond to any of his Academy Level techniques, he became visibly frustrated and let the "bad cop" role slip too early with a mean hard stare. From my experience, I knew the "bad cop" routine needs to be built up gradually to be believed; the "good cop" can play his role from the "get-go." The FDLE agent built rapport, followed the book and his attempts at positive contact were rewarded with friendly responses each time. However, Mr. F.B.I. couldn't quite understand why his intimidation technique was falling flat. I could have told him why.

It never occurred to him that his condescending tone and plan to instill fear was a miscalculation because of *who* he was interviewing. As a street cop I had experienced contact with many types of hard-talking, intimidating groups known for violence; biker groups, street gangs, ethnic neighborhood factions who would like nothing more than to cause a law enforcement officer great bodily harm. I was not going to be bullied or intimidated.

I would probably say 99% of all street cops who handle volatile people and situations daily may look at these "politician FBI agents" as basically desk jockeys. I'm fully aware that some F.B.I. agents are capable of conducting wonderfully magnificent and productive interviews, but most high-ranking political special agents need to allow true field personnel (often referred to as brick agents because they pounded the pavement regularly) to obtain needed information. The skill of conducting interrogations is a perishable one over time if not practiced on live subjects in real-life situations. I can only surmise that the FDLE agent sensed the uncomfortable vibe and clearly adjusted the quickest.

Feeling a bit like I may have hurt some feelings, I allowed the FDLE agent to get away with the next generic direction of the interview, "In your own words and in any way you wish to present it, explain your relationship with George and your involvement in this case."

Normally, criminals and interrogators battle over every jealously guarded answer and there are back-and-forth exchanges designed to wear the other down. However, I was not a criminal and being armed with nothing but the truth, I freely explained the relationship between George and me. Evidently, my interviewers wanted more than my boring version of the truth.

They then applied a slight "direction through suggestion" technique, but hit a brick wall. They fished for any damning information about George that could be used against him in the upcoming trial. Two and a half hours into the interview, they dropped the indirect appeal and a more direct assault was made.

"Did you know that when George was arrested in Jacksonville, he had a handgun that held over 20 rounds of assault rifle type ammunition in his possession?"

Their question to me was followed by a few seconds of silence. I knew this was a "Hail Mary" pass to get me to agree that this could indicate George was an out of control madman, intent on vigilante justice.

"The handgun you are describing is my gun. It is the FNH-57." This gun is ahead of its time as a paper target destroyer and admired by the combat handgun world. "I gave it to George," I answered unflinchingly.

"Don't you think it was irresponsible of you to give such a man as George Zimmerman a handgun after what happened on February 26th?"

I felt the anger rising, but remained calm. "What right do you have to suggest my conduct was irresponsible, when George was a free man? He is cooperating fully with detectives, and the police had returned his concealed weapons permit."

Then, I unleashed what I had been holding in since it had been made known that the Black Panthers had set a price on George's head. "Furthermore, it is far more irresponsible to have video evidence of a racially motivated terrorist leader placing a $10,000 dead or alive bounty on George, and not one action was taken against him. That is cowardice, if you ask me.

"No one in the Trayvon Martin family, and no one in the black community, uttered a word of displeasure or condemnation of such a blatant, disturbing threat. No one in the justice department has announced any action to be taken against the so-called New Black Panther organization or its leader following the 'dead or alive' offer. Talk about irresponsible." I was on a roll, and I just couldn't keep silent any longer.

"While this death threat goes unnoticed, the justice department is trying to build a hate-crime case against my friend, and it is chugging along with blinders on."

I knew my chances of ever getting transferred to the F.B.I. were now in severe jeopardy, but I had to say what was right instead of what was personally profitable. I needed to stay true to the direction in which I had steered George since the first day he ever asked my opinion. Any other course of action would have labeled me as a coward myself – one of the worst words I can use toward people of such character.

I have always maintained that truth can overcome anything. Then, even if you are brought low by any circumstance, you will still claim dignity from "fighting the good fight" of faith. Certain values shouldn't be compromised, even unto death. I pray often that in any situation I will have the strength and divine fortitude to live up to these words.

The voluntary interview with the F.B.I. and the Florida Department of Law Enforcement abruptly ended after I spoke at length about these strong convictions.

# Chapter 7

## George Re-Arrested, Along with Shellie — Didn't Need That!

*Mark*

Neither George or Shellie Zimmerman returned to our home after April 21st when George was released on bail. Shellie's father stopped by to pick up clothes and a few other items they had left behind at the house. That was near the end of May. I'm sure he delivered them to George and Shellie wherever they were staying up north. We had no chance to say good-bye to our friends. Sondra and Shellie continued to text each other often, and Shellie would relay our messages of support to George. We have not spoken to George directly since the day he was first taken into custody.

Then, just hours after rejoicing over George's release from jail on bond, word came that a new arrest warrant had been issued because the Zimmermans had misled the court regarding their financial situation. This time Shellie was involved and also facing charges. So, just when things couldn't get worse ... they did.

On April 20, 2012, George's first bond hearing was held. These types of hearings are used to ascertain whether a criminal defendant is a flight risk, and to establish his or her finances and set a bond accordingly. A judge sets bond at an amount that will discourage flight and guarantee the defendant's presence at a later trial.

At George's hearing, Shellie testified by phone. When asked about their finances, she told the court that both she and her husband were unemployed, and she was still in nursing school. The implication was that their financial situation was dire, and there was little money for his defense. Bond was set at $150,000, and George was released on April 23.

However, at a separate and unrelated hearing on April 27, George's attorney, Mark O'Mara, disclosed that the Zimmermans had raised over $200,000 in donations on a personal website founded on April 9. O'Mara claimed he had learned of the money while shutting down the website with George.

O'Mara acknowledged that at least $135,000 was accessible to the Zimmermans at the time of the bond hearing. Therefore, prosecutors said, Shellie Zimmerman had lied under oath. O'Mara called it an "oversight" and assured the court that the money had been transferred to a defense fund out of the Zimmermans' control.

Here was the problem. On June 1, the prosecution presented recorded prison phone calls between Shellie and George in which the two had discussed their finances. In the calls, George had brought up "Peter Pan" repeatedly—a reference, the prosecution said, to PayPal, the website where his donations were being processed. The couple had talked about money in amounts of $10 and $20, which the prosecution said was code for $10,000 and $20,000. There had also been discussions in the calls about how to move this money between their bank accounts. Bank records show several such transfers.

The case's presiding judge, Circuit Judge Kenneth Lester Jr., agreed the Zimmermans had misrepresented themselves, and George's bond was revoked. He ordered George to return to jail within 48 hours. He complied immediately and turned himself in, once again.

So, Shellie was arrested for perjury on June 12th. She was released on $1,000 bond the same day, and her arraignment date was set for July 31st. On July 27th, she entered a written not guilty plea. She waived her right to appear at the arraignment. At the time of this writing there had been no date set for hearing.

Several of the prison phone calls between the Zimmermans were released on June 18th, to much media attention, of course. On the recorded calls, George is heard discussing the money with both Shellie and his brother-in-law. I wish I could have had the opportunity to advise George how every recorded conversation would be dissected and analyzed and used against him if possible.

George's *second* bond hearing was held on June 29. Here, O'Mara emphasized that the money had been transferred to a third party, and pointed out that the defendant (George) had made no attempt to flee while on bond. He had turned himself in promptly, O'Mara said. The prosecution, however, said Zimmerman had purposefully hidden the money and deceived the court outright. Prosecutor Bernie de la Rionda called for George to stay in jail until his trial.

The judge considered the evidence over several days, and then on July 5th, set the new bond at $1 million; quite a jump from the original amount. Lester wrote in his decision, "It is entirely reasonable for this court to find that, but for the requirement that he be placed on electronic monitoring, the defendant and his wife would have fled the United States with at least $130,000 of other people's money."

On July 6, George posted bond yet again and was released. The new terms of the release stated he could not travel, could not open a bank account, and could not obtain a passport. He would be electronically monitored, and has a 6 p.m. to 6 a.m. curfew. George's attorney reported there was at least $211,000 in their defense fund as of July 5th.

For me, it all comes down to this question: Did Shelly lie on purpose regarding the money they had on hand? By the way, in my opinion, it was an ill-advised move, no matter how you look at it. Even if it was some kind of misunderstanding about the defense funds, George or Shellie didn't tell the "whole truth." It just looked bad.

The prosecution didn't care so much about fingering Shellie; they wanted it to be a slam against George's character. Their motive was clear: *if he lied about this, he may have lied about the shooting of Trayvon Martin.*

# Chapter 8

Is George Zimmerman a Racist?

*Mark*

As George awaits trial, many people have formed an opinion as to whether or not he racially profiled Trayvon Martin on the night of the shooting that took the young man's life. Many believe George made racially motivated comments when he called 911 to report a young black male who seemed suspicious, and in George's words, looked like he was "up to no good." Many are convinced that George was guilty of racial profiling because Trayvon was black and wearing a hoodie that night, and those two things alone caused George to perceive him to be suspicious.

Then, included in the 911 call which George made from the townhome complex, many believe he is heard making a racial slur. Some voice analysts insist George mutters, "fucking coons." He maintains that he is saying "punks," referencing previous incidents in the area.

We've already mentioned that George didn't immediately offer the information that the person he was reporting as suspicious was a young black male. The police officer asked a direct question during the call, "Okay, and this guy – is he black, white or Hispanic?"

To which George replied, "He looks black."

That's it. Those three words were uttered and George was presumed guilty of profiling, following, and murdering Trayvon Martin.

The George Zimmerman we know is *not* a racist. He's half-white, half-Latino himself. Hispanics also have a shared history of being victims of racial tension. George's father commented in an interview, "He (George) would be the last to discriminate for any reason whatsoever." He added, "George was more like the boy who died, because he was a minority, too."

## Sondra

One family member of George's sent a letter (actually a plea) to the NAACP President, Turner Clayton, addressing this issue:

*"It's time for you to end the race issue in this matter and call for cooler heads to prevail. If something happens to George as a result of the race furor stirred up by this mischaracterization of George, there will be blood on your hands as well as the other racists who have rushed to judgment. You need to call off the dogs. Period. Publically and swiftly ... George has been called a racist and a bigot and there have been very few that have stood up for him."*

The letter goes on to mention that George was one of very few people in Sanford, Florida, who spoke out publically to condemn the beating of a black homeless man by the son of a Sanford police officer. *"Do you know the individual who stepped up when no one in the black community would? Do you know who spent tireless hours putting flyers on the cars of parked cars in churches within the black community seeking justice for the man? Do you know who waited on churchgoers to exit so he could personally hand them the information in at attempt to organize the black community against this horrible miscarriage of justice? Do you know who helped organize the City Hall Meeting regarding the case on January 8, 2011? That person was George Zimmerman."*

Ironic, isn't it? The George Zimmerman we know never implied or spoke one word of prejudice or racism.

### Mark

George introduced me to many of his friends who were black, and he had several. I have witnessed personally their interaction, mutual respect, and genuine admiration. Once, a black friend of George met the four of us (George and Shellie and me and Sondra) at a restaurant. In an effort to make sure the friend didn't feel left out because he was single, George drew him in to our conversations, and we were delighted to get to know him. The way he and George interacted, you'd have thought they had known each other since childhood. He had other awesome black friends, and I never observed the tiniest hint of prejudice in George. He was as comfortable relating to them as he was with me.

When all of the protest marches were underway following the shooting and black crowds gathered to call for George's arrest, he asked me on more than one occasion, "Should we call some of my black friends and ask them to make a statement or form a protest march of their own in support of me?"

Of course, at that time serious death threats surfaced and we didn't want any of those friends to suffer repercussions. I think one of the most serious incidents occurred when black Hollywood director, Spike Lee, tweeted an address purported to be the house where George was staying at the time. The information was not correct and the outcome of that senseless, hate-filled report could have been disastrous for the people living at the reported address who had no idea their lives were in danger. Lee later apologized, but just the idea that someone would be that irresponsible is mind-boggling to me. Actually, it could be considered downright criminal, but absolutely nothing was done to Spike Lee in response to this blatantly racially motivated act.

*Sondra*

As a Florida native, I understand there can be racial tension, but here's the thing. The state is made up of people all mixed-up race-wise. Friends I knew in school had Hispanic names like Gonzales or Manuel, but they couldn't speak a word of Spanish, and then the whitest kids I knew went around speaking perfect French, or Spanish, or Italian. It's all over the place. George is not dark-skinned or light, but sort of light brown. His mother was born in Peru. There was not one element of racism that entered into the tragic shooting of Trayvon Martin on the rainy night of February 26th. George or Trayvon could have been green and the outcome would have been the same. There was a tragic encounter, but it is a case of self defense – nothing more.

### Mark

There is no doubt in my mind that when the case goes to trial, the prosecution will strongly insinuate that George was racially motivated to follow and confront Trayvon Martin. I use the term "insinuate," because I don't know how they could prove that was his state of mind that night inside Twin Lakes. It will be up to a jury to decide if George Zimmerman shot an unarmed teenager due to racial prejudice. It may all come down to a matter of interpretation as to whether Trayvon's civil rights were violated. George's fate may rest on how his defense reacts to pieced together evidence or innuendo, analyzed recordings of the 911 call, and whatever the court allows or disallows.

I hope someone mentions George's civil rights, too. The fundamental basic right of anyone to defend themselves in (real or perceived real) life-threatening situations cannot be overlooked. Talk about a miscarriage of justice. I don't know what direction at this juncture George's attorneys will take. Many think Florida's "stand your ground" law will be used in George's defense. I just never thought it would get this far. Still hard for me to believe there will even be an actual trial. This one thing I know – George Zimmerman did not racially profile, follow, then murder Trayvon Martin. It simply was *not* in my best friend's character.

# Chapter 9

## Public Outcry Demanded George Be Charged...with Something

It was breaking news across the country. George Zimmerman, our best friend, has been charged with second degree murder. Here is the law as defined by Florida Statute:

To prove second degree murder, a prosecutor must show that the defendant acted according to a "depraved mind" without regard for human life. Florida state laws permit the prosecution of second degree murder when the killing lacked premeditation or planning, but the defendant acted with enmity toward the victim or the two had an ongoing interaction or relationship. Unlike first degree murder, second degree murder does not necessarily require proof of the defendant's intent to kill.

Second degree murder is the most serious charge they could bring against George, given that premeditation (required for a first degree murder charge) was completely out of the question in this case. Sentences for second degree murder vary from state to state. If found guilty in Florida George could face the maximum sentence of life in prison, or a sentence anywhere from one year up to 30 years. Parole requirements and actual time served varies from state to state also, so we do not know the exact amount of time George would spend in prison if found guilty.

In our opinion, George's trial, whenever it takes place, will most likely focus on eight areas:

1. **The Prosecution Wants to Portray George as a Racist**

    The prosecutor will try to show that George acted out of racial prejudice by profiling, following, then shooting young Trayvon Martin to death. As discussed previously, we *know* our friend is not a racist. The flyer he distributed around town which called for justice for a black homeless man beaten by a police officer's son speaks volumes. On that flyer, George included the famous quote by Edmund Burke, "The only thing necessary for the triumph of evil, is that good men do nothing."

George felt compelled to do something so he took those words to heart. In that instance, he spent his money, his time, and even put his safety in jeopardy to be a "good man" who did something. Here he is now, on trial because many in our society demanded he be charged, not on the basis of fact or evidence, but because it made good copy and spiked up television news ratings to make the shooting something more than a simple case of self defense.

This is entertainment at the highest level for many people. The story keeps "racial" issues stirred up, and it doesn't hurt the smiling, even chipper prosecutor who hopes the case will bring in cash for her re-election campaign and perhaps a book offer.

Even when it was discovered that George was not a snarling, white supremacist with a shaved head, but a man of Latin descent, the media labeled him, not as Hispanic, but a "*white* Hispanic." Our friend has been charged with shooting a young black man, and the state will try to depict George as the face of deep-seeded racism that still exists in America. Nothing could be further from the truth.

The prosecuting attorneys will try to say the 911 recordings reveal that George uttered a racial slur during the call he made on February 26th. This will be difficult to prove, due to the barely audible words, but still the idea will be implanted in the minds of the jurors that it was *possibly* racial name-calling. We believe George when he said he did not use the derogatory term. As we affirmed in a previous chapter, George and Shellie had many black friends and we never saw any hint of prejudice in the man.

We imagine George thinks this has all been a huge mistake, a nightmare that will soon be over. He thinks this because he is *not* a racist, therefore, not guilty. Sooner or later, he is sure everyone will know the truth. It is just a matter of time. What our friend may not understand fully is that he has been chosen to serve as representative of white, gun-toting racists who feel a right to follow black teenagers wandering around in their gated communities; and he's the sacrificial lamb.

## 2. Prosecutors will Portray George Zimmerman as a "Cowboy Vigilante" Making Up His Own Rules

As a back-up plan to the prosecutions' intent to paint George as a racist, they will also try to imply that his motives were not only racially motivated, but also driven by a desire for power, significance, or control. Much has been made of George being a "self appointed neighborhood watchman." Did George see himself as the neighborhood "protector"? Did he appoint himself a volunteer watchman to meet a need for recognition, to be seen as a hero? Was he seeking acceptance, or validation through serving as a "look out" for trouble at The Retreat at Twin Lakes?

Prosecution will be able to prove that George called the police over 46 times since 2004. In itself and on the surface it would seem that George was "overzealous" about reporting anything and everything to the police, including open garage doors to suspicious characters, several of whom were black. As pointed out previously, however, many of George's neighbors within The Retreat made George their contact, and then he in turn called the police on their behalf. So, he was just being a caring and concerned neighbor which does not make him "territorial" or "over protective" as he has been portrayed in the press. And, certainly it doesn't make him a murderer. The George Zimmerman we know is not an out-of-control vigilante type. Instead, he is extremely mild mannered, respectful, and caring.

3. **The Prosecution May Suggest that George Was "Hyper-Vigilant" Due to Recent Crime in the Neighborhood**

Was George experiencing a heightened sense of fear on the night of February 26$^{th}$ due to previous crimes in the neighborhood? If so, he took it upon himself to follow Trayvon and overreacted to his presence, thus causing the confrontation and consequent shooting. This could be an argument that surfaces and actually could benefit both sides. The prosecutor could claim he was extremely fearful and leery of suspicious "blacks" due to recent criminal activity; the defense could argue the reason he reported Trayvon as suspicious was *because* of the many crimes reported in recent months leading up to the shooting. Several neighbors reported they were on edge due to the string of robberies. We will see how it plays out.

## 4. The "Stand Your Ground" Law May Provide Some Protection from Prosecution

Many believed, especially just following the arrest, that George's defense strategy would depend heavily on Florida's so called "stand your ground" law. The law, passed in 2005, states that a person can use deadly force if he or she believes it is "necessary to do so to prevent death or great bodily harm to himself, or another, or to prevent the commission of a forcible felony."

To date, it seems more likely that George's defense team will go with a simple self defense argument. Many prosecutors across the country have the opinion that the "stand your ground" law is too broad in defining when a person is actually in imminent danger. Since its passing, they believe there have been too many so-called "justified homicides" that may have been closer to murder, but this law has protected the perpetrator.

The problem we see in using the "stand your ground" defense in George's case is that usually the person claiming it is the person being pursued, not the person doing the pursuing, as many believe George was doing that night.

The prosecution will interject that George was looking for Trayvon that night, in fact, following him; therefore, he initiated the confrontation, and the deadly struggle ensued.

This is a question that will most likely never be fully resolved. Who was the aggressor when both Trayvon and George came face to face? We believe George spoke the truth when he said he was headed back to his car when Trayvon approached him and instigated the physical fight. George was not trying to do the job of the police that evening. He was doing what he thought he should: observing and reporting potential crime. George had no choice but to defend himself. A terrible tragedy, yes, but the shooting is a clear case of self defense.

## 5. Why Did George Zimmerman Continue to Follow Trayvon Martin after the Police Directed Him Otherwise? Why Didn't Zimmerman Identify Himself to Trayvon?

You can believe these points will be brought up at trial. Our take is simple – we choose to believe George. He said he was not "following" Trayvon, but was walking to the next street sign so he could direct the police to his position within the complex. Then, while George was returning to his car, Trayvon confronted him. As to why George didn't identify himself to Trayvon, there may have been several reasons.

Perhaps, there was no time for George to identify himself. As the incident was reported, George said Trayvon almost immediately knocked him to the ground. Could be that it just didn't occur to George as the situation escalated to try and declare who he was and why he was there. It is easy for us to say, in hindsight, "Well, George should have told Trayvon immediately who he was and that he was looking out for the neighborhood." George may have perceived that announcing his position, or trying to tell Trayvon why he was there, was not going to quell the young man's anger. If George had identified himself as a neighborhood watch volunteer, we don't believe it would have made a difference in the outcome.

## 6. The Gun

Many residents, some of whom support George's actions of February 26th, do not think it was wise that he carried a concealed weapon that night. "If there had not been a gun, Trayvon and George may have come out of the skirmish roughed up a bit, but no one would be dead," they surmised.

This much we know. George's gun was legal. He had a legal license for it and a license to conceal it. It is a constitutional right for citizens to be armed. He was going to the grocery store, he wasn't "strapping it on" to join a posse or look for trouble. The gun was part of George's normal attire; some may not understand or approve, but it is a guaranteed right under the laws of the United States.

This is a major crux of the case. Did George indeed believe he was in a life or death struggle with Trayvon Martin? George's testimony is that Trayvon was trying to suffocate him after banging his head into the sidewalk and breaking his nose. He never thought or intended that his gun would be needed, or used on the evening of February 26th, but we believe it saved his life.

### 7. The Phone Call From Trayvon's Girlfriend

In the moments leading up to the shooting of Trayvon Martin, the teenager had been on the phone with his girlfriend. Phone records verify that at approximately 7:12 P.M. Trayvon's cell phone rang and he spoke to his girlfriend on his headset as he walked between the rows of townhouses of The Retreat at Twin Lakes. He was returning from a trip to a nearby convenience store where he purchased a bag of Skittles and a can of Arizona Tea. Because it was chilly and beginning to rain, he pulled a gray hoodie up over his head.

Almost immediately Trayvon tells the girlfriend that a "strange man" is watching him. She tells him, "Run."

The next thing she hears is Trayvon's voice asking, "What are you following me for?"

Another voice asks, "What are you doing here?"

Then, the sounds of the scuffle between George and Trayvon can be heard before Trayvon's phone goes silent. The time now is 7:16 when many hear someone screaming for help, then report a gun shot. The first policeman arrives on the scene only one minute later to find Trayvon unresponsive.

The prosecution and defense will most likely go back and forth as to whether the phone call should be entered as evidence. George's defense team will say, "It is hearsay."

The prosecutor will argue the call should be admitted because they are the words of a dying man, a "dying declaration" if you will, which is allowed in

Defending our Friend | 149

court in some cases. Of course, the prosecution is going to have a hard time proving Trayvon was in the process of dying before the phone went dead. Our guess is that the prosecution will get it in somehow, to produce jury sympathy if nothing else.

Trayvon's parents appeared on the *Today* show and stated their opinion regarding the girlfriend's phone call. "It proves that Trayvon wasn't doing anything wrong. It proves that he wasn't walking around the neighborhood doing anything suspicious. He was on his way home," his dad said.

However, since reading up on the case, we have learned that the trip from the convenience store back to where Trayvon was staying on February 26th should have been a much shorter trip. Evidently he did not go straight home after leaving the store. What exactly was he doing from the time he left the store to the time George notices him? Was he simply taking his time, wandering aimlessly, or was there something more sinister in his actions? Could the young man have been scoping out homes along the way for a possible burglary opportunity? We will never know.

What we do know is that even after Trayvon notices George, he doesn't return to the townhome immediately. We will never know why. From the start of the 911 call George made to the police at 7 p.m., Trayvon had about five minutes to walk to the townhome where he was staying. From the mailboxes by the clubhouse where George started his call to the townhome was only some 800 feet. If running, Trayvon could have made it to his front door in a minute. If walking, it would have taken him two minutes.

By no means are we saying the young man was definitely doing anything sinister; it is just interesting that Trayvon didn't choose to get home right away after noticing George. There are various reasons possible. He could have just been taking his time, not in a hurry to get back; perhaps he didn't want this stranger to discover where he was staying; he was running around trying to avoid him; he didn't want to be cornered or trapped; or the other possibility that many will not want to hear – that Trayvon feared the motive behind his "suspicious behavior" was discovered, and he thought someone would hold him there for the cops to arrive. So, he was running between the buildings, not along the main sidewalk. Again, we will never know.

Two specific questions are indicative of the public's perception of Trayvon:

Was he the kid who confronts George when George is returning to his car, asking, "Do you have a fucking problem?" To which George responds, "No." Trayvon comes back with, "Well, you do now."

Or, is he the teen in the hoodie who turns to Zimmerman and asks simply, "Why are you following me?"

The prosecution's goal will be to portray George as the aggressor, the hunter who stalked a young unarmed teenager. That is not the George Zimmerman we know.

## 8. The Voice Heard Pleading for Help

The recordings of eight calls made to the police on the night of the shooting were released on March 17, 2012. By now, thousands of people have listened to them. They are chilling no matter what side you are on in this case. If you listen, you will hear a voice pleading for help; you will also hear the gunshot; only one.

We believe George is the one heard on the calls crying out for help. This will be an important battle line for both sides during the trial. One eyewitness will testify it was Zimmerman calling for help as Trayvon was on top of him beating his head into the paved sidewalk. There is another witness, who heard but did not see the shooting, who believes Trayvon was the one calling for help.

The *Orlando Sentinel* reported earlier that two forensic voice specialists determined that the screams in the background of the 911 recordings were *not* from Zimmerman. Trayvon's mother is absolutely sure that the voice calling for help is the voice of her son. It has been reported that other testing done by police confirms it is George's voice.

I think there will be a lot of argument as to whether or not voiceprint analysis is reliable and admissible as evidence. We'll see. Of course, comments have been made by the media noting that even if the calls verify it was George calling for help, it wouldn't mean Trayvon was less vulnerable at that moment. Trayvon could have been focused on escaping, or surviving instead of calling for help. George has never wavered in this regard; we believe it is his voice plaintively calling for help several times. To us, the real shame is that no one responded. Someone possibly could have helped to stop the fight that ended so tragically. No one came forward in response to those chilling screams in the night.

It may be months, even a year or more, before the case comes to trial. We are very aware, however, that our good friend is already guilty in the minds of millions. We are extremely troubled by a system that can accuse anyone, regardless of the basic facts of the case, send him and his family scurrying underground in fear of their lives, then try him in the court of public opinion without regard to his crushed dreams, a reputation he will never shake, not to mention the very real possibility he will pay and has already paid for just being a responsible citizen, a helpful neighbor who tried to do the right thing.

We have sadly concluded that George cannot win. No matter the outcome of the trial, whether found guilty or innocent, he will lose. A guilty verdict would take from him any possible hope for a normal life. Every dream he and Shellie had in regard to how they planned to live their lives would be crushed in an instant. Of course, those things may be gone already. Incarceration of any length would take a toll on his health and psyche, and on the relationships he holds dear. If a jury finds him guilty, his name would be forever linked to the senseless killing of an unarmed teenager. Worst of all he will be viewed as an out-of-control gun waver whose prejudice and hate caused him to shoot the defenseless teen.

If George is found innocent, the consequences could be even more costly. He will be blamed for possible nationwide racial unrest, riots, threats of uprisings, and widespread violence. He would be the cause for a major setback of racial relations in our country and ostracized by both the black and white communities as a social pariah. Even with an innocent verdict, the stigma produced by the case will swallow him whole.

We do not know at this point whether we will be called to testify at George's trial. Certainly, we want to help in George's defense if possible. Our one hope, which we must hold to, is in a God who promises to grant His children peace, purpose, and the promise of a new tomorrow. The Bible clearly states, with God all things are possible. We pray for that better tomorrow for George and Shellie. We miss our friends and look forward to telling them so.

# Chapter 10

## Closer Than a Brother

"There are friends who pretend to be friends, but there is a friend who sticks closer than a brother."

Proverbs 18:24

It's always there: the possibility our best friend could go to jail for a very long time, and it makes us feel utterly helpless. We liken these days leading up to George's trial to holding your breath underwater. You can do it pretty well for just so long and then, you must have air. Our hope is, after the trial is over, that we, the Zimmermans, and all who believe in George's innocence, will be able to breathe again without all this constant pressure, drama, and fear.

We experience two warring emotions about George's situation: One, we strive to continue to pray and trust

Almighty God with the entire situation; the judge, the attorneys, the jury, the witnesses, and yes, even the verdict. The second emotion is a deep boiling fury just below the surface that we strive to control almost moment to moment. It is the fury only a street cop who has seen countless horrible acts of injustice can know.

Should George be convicted of the charges against him, could we contain our anger? Not without supernatural help. Even drug addicts, gamblers, or serious alcoholics will tell you they must depend on a "higher power" or a "divine source" for strength. If the jury returns a guilty verdict for George, we will need God to show up big time for us. We believe in his innocence that much. It is faith that has brought us and George and Shellie Zimmerman this far; He will help us as we see this through to the end. He will even help us forgive those who have ruthlessly sought to destroy the most gentle and sincerely kind man we have ever known.

Whenever the trial gets underway, it's sure to be another "circus." Florida proceedings are open to the public so George's trial will be televised and covered heavily by the media. It comes with being famous we suppose. Andy Warhol stated that everyone will have fifteen minutes of fame. But this is a fame George would have never sought for himself. The word *famous* is dangerously close to the word *infamous,* a word we fear may follow George for the rest of his life. Never in his wildest imagination could he have thought an event in his life would spark national debates on racial profiling, gun control, and self defense issues. At times, it almost seems as if he doesn't quite understand himself what is going on or the possible consequences.

Daniel Greenfield, a New York City freelance commentator who writes on political issues wrote a column regarding George's plight. In the article he mentioned "the very randomness of choosing Zimmerman, the contempt of the basic facts of the case, has become part of the message." He goes on to add: "The message is the same. The facts don't matter. The decision-making process doesn't matter. Leave your evidence home … and watch how the wheels spin, the gears grind and the blood flows. The message is that the system is absolute and there is no escape.

"This is evil. It is the very essence of evil. It is an evil that Zimmerman could not have seen coming or understood when he was out patrolling his community. It's an evil that is all around us. We can catch glimpses of it on the evening news, in the sneers of anchormen, the practiced smiles of politicians, it's there in Angela Corey's (the State's prosecutor) helpless grin, it's there in the mountains of paperwork, the lines of tiny print, the lines of people waiting at bullet proof windows, the morality mobs forming up digitally for the next victim to string up, the next popular opinion to enforce, the next skull to crush."

We agree with Mr. Greenfield's powerfully written commentary. There is a reality show mentality out there trying to grab attention any way they can, even when based on lies and half truths. The media just shrugs and lets it happen because ratings are involved. George Zimmerman became a victim of the world we live in. He's "the story" right now, until the next one comes along.

In the days before George's arrest, protestors marched under banners demanding, "Justice for Trayvon." They chose a slogan: "I am Trayvon." Those words began to appear on T-shirts, hats, and especially on hoodies. The words were a statement to show that any black person could be a victim like Trayvon, who, as they chimed, was "killed just for being black and walking around in a gated community."

Perhaps, as George awaits trial, it's time to start a similar campaign: "I am George Zimmerman." Truly, any one of us could have been in our car, headed out to do a simple errand, on that rainy night in Sanford, Florida. We could have behaved exactly as George did when he noticed the young black male looking into a window of a residence.

He called the police just to ask them to check it out. The only thing different is that George carried a gun; most of us do not. For that fact, and especially for the fact that he used the gun to defend himself, he has been demonized by sports figures, movie stars, politicians, and even the President, who suggested if he had a son, he would have "looked like Trayvon."

We are all George Zimmerman to a certain extent, and not one of us can say what we would have done in George's situation. "Oh, I would have never pulled my gun!" Really? You know that for certain, even when someone else was trying to grab the gun from you? George believed he or Trayvon was going to die that evening as they both struggled for the weapon.

I am George Zimmerman because I may have chosen to do the same thing. In the same situation, I would try to get control of my gun and protect myself, before the other guy takes it from me and ends my life. We are all only a tiny step away from being George Zimmerman at any time.

This case has changed all of us connected to George and Shellie Zimmerman. In July of 2012, the *Miami Herald* contacted us requesting an interview. We declined. Of course, they proceeded to write the article anyway. Mark's position within the Department of Homeland Security has been compromised due to their careless reporting. The *Herald* was given access to Mark's interview with the FBI and Florida Department of Law Enforcement and excerpts were published without our comments or any verification from us. Other requests have come, but we will continue to be very cautious as the trial date approaches.

In August we were contacted by the producers of the Dr. Phil television program requesting that we appear on the popular program. We both immediately felt our appearance on the show, would provide the public with a more positive glimpse into the heart and character of George Zimmerman, the friend we grew to know and love. We flew to Los Angeles and taped the show on August 22$^{nd}$. The program was scheduled to air in mid September.

Of course, we had some nervous jitters as the show began. This was a national stage neither one of us ever envisioned would be available to us just a few months back. We expected there would be some tough questions thrown to us through out the interview: questions we knew the viewing public would be asking. Dr. Phil runs his show unscripted, unrehearsed and completely in a no-nonsense style. If we were not prepared to respond to the inquiries or unable to portray George as the friend and brother we love, then we needed to stay home. Instead, we answered honestly and as transparently as possible, every single question. The Dr. Phil show allowed us to present our passion and insight into George's character in the most respectful and dignified ways. Trayvon Martin's step mother also appeared on the program and we expressed to her our sincere sympathy and condolences for the loss of their loved one.

The people who produce Dr. Phil's show are consummate professionals. They were respectful, helpful, and at every level they radiated a calm, even perspective that allowed us to complete the important task at hand with a sense of calm, also. We were privileged to meet Robin McGraw, Dr. Phil's wife, and she spoke genuine caring words, which reassured us as we prepared for the taping of the show.

For us, Dr. Phil himself became more than the television celebrity we had followed for years. He was the same off stage as on, the real deal and an amazing man of character. We spoke later of the many damaged souls who had sought Dr. Phil's help, their lives in complete ruin, only to be given wise counsel and effective tools with which they could rebuild and heal. He has the distinct gift of giving people hope. He and Robin truly want to make the world a little bit better than they find it. What kind of world could we create if we all tried to follow their example? We deeply appreciate the opportunity, the time, the platform, and the unforgettable experience to appear on the show. I'm sure there will be some interest in the book and perhaps more interview requests will come after the show is aired.

We expect people to question our motives for writing this book. Some will call us opportunists, shameless money-grabbers trying to profit from our friend's notoriety, his misfortune. For the record, we did not receive an advance from the publisher of this book. Not one cent has been exchanged or promised to us in terms of guaranteed sales, or marketing schemes. Our goals from the beginning have been very simple:

1) To come to the defense of a friend who has been portrayed in the court of public opinion to be someone he is not. We wanted to be the voice no one has heard. The first voice to publically state that George Zimmerman is not a racist, a control freak, or a gun-toting, chest-beating, "clean up the town" cowboy bent on getting all the bad guys. He values life, and is a decent, hard-working, frugal, funny, loving son, brother, and husband, and a good, good friend. The shooting at Twin Lakes was nothing more than a chance encounter that went horribly wrong; but it wasn't murder.

2) We also wanted to express what we believe are the elements that define the characteristics of a true, long-

lasting, loyal, committed friendship, the likes of which we enjoyed with George and Shellie Zimmerman.

There is a long process ahead for George and Shellie. After this trial, there may be a federal trial, also. The federal investigation will focus on whether or not the shooting was racially motivated and if George denied Trayvon Martin's civil rights. Whether or not a federal trial will proceed will be determined largely by the outcome of Florida's criminal trial.

We were blessed to have George and Shellie Zimmerman as close friends. Some people go through their entire lives wishing they had a close friend. Others go through life keeping people at a distance, determined to not let anyone close. How sad. Our times with the Zimmermans were some of the happiest times we have ever known. Whether it was spending time at the gun range or meeting George and Shellie for a meal out, enjoying their company during the holidays, or laughing over inside jokes, we had a unique and special bond. We observed our daughter's friendship with George, too. He showed genuine interest in all she was doing and celebrated her biggest or smallest accomplishments. She loves him and misses him. She has often asked, "When will we see George and Shellie again?" We don't know the answer to that question.

Even if we had not been good friends we would have admired and appreciated George for the respect and character he exhibited. We valued George and Shellie in our lives and hope one day our friendship can be fully restored. We had long talks about many subjects with the Zimmermans, but more importantly, we learned through the years to listen to each other. We listened not just to answer, but we listened to understand each other's opinions, hurts, joys, and dreams for the future. We deeply regret the circumstances that took George and Shellie away from us.

There was unconditional acceptance between the Ostermans and the Zimmermans. We felt George especially needed the emotional support of another man he could pour his heart out to. We tried not to lecture, but when asked, we would offer the lessons we had learned from life. Mark was accused of coaching George before George was interviewed by the police. When asked about that directly, during the interview on April 26th with the FBI and the Florida Department of Law Enforcement, Mark answered immediately, "The only advice I gave him was to tell the truth." With our whole hearts we believe George has done that – told the truth about the incident with Trayvon Martin.

George was looking forward to a fulfilling marriage and the kind of home he and Shellie wanted to build together. They were on their way. He spoke often of pursuing an education that would lead to more opportunities for his family. We hosted a graduation party for him just days before the shooting. He was close to earning his associate's degree in criminal justice (a course away) at Seminole State College. Then, when the shooting occurred, he was immediately expelled. Many of their dreams are on hold, if not completely shattered.

I believe it is a strong indication of George's character that he has attempted to apologize to the Martin family at every opportunity. Their first reaction was to comment that the apology was "insincere," "fake," "contrived." We know differently. George was and is devastated by the death of a young man who had his whole life ahead of him. We have seen the tears, the wrenching sorrow as he tried to express his sadness over the event that led to the shooting of Trayvon Martin. We know about the many sleepless nights, the sincere sympathy he felt for Trayvon's family. He understood their hurt, their anger, their desire for answers. We have prayed together with George that Trayvon's family will be comforted and they would know a peace that passes understanding: the peace only God can grant.

If a guilty verdict is returned, George and Shellie's fate will be determined by the court. We honestly hope that we have interaction with them once the trial is over, no matter the verdict. We would love to build upon the rapport, the easy relationship, the unspoken connection that marked our friendship in so many ways. As stated, we don't know if that would be possible. It would be our joy to hope with each other again, to laugh, to cry, to know their children, for George to see Breanna grow into a lovely young lady with children of her own, to sit on someone's porch when we are old and recall these hard, hard days. If we never re-connect with George, or even if we never hear from him and Shellie again, we will understand, although it will be hard. Our friendship with George and Shellie Zimmerman has produced enough great times and memories to last a lifetime. We thank them from our hearts.

We are probably correct in projecting that should George be found innocent, the couple will want to stay far away from Florida. The reminders of February 26$^{th}$, his worst nightmare, would be too close, too painful. Plus, the interest and pressure from the media would be much more intense. They may choose to settle somewhere across the country, or even out of the country, since his name will always be linked to a case that will remain an American tragedy. We can only imagine the desire would be strong to separate your life into two categories: Everything that happened before February 26th, and everything that happened after. We are part of the world he knew *before* that awful night. Nothing would remain the same; how could it? We get that.

However, it was on that awful night, the most difficult night George will ever know, he leaned hard on our friendship and we were there. From the night of Shellie's call on February 26th, to today, we have been fully engaged and 100% supportive of our friends. We will be there for the trial, the aftermath, and throughout any fallout the verdict produces. Because that is what friends do.

We have heard some talking heads say that George's trial will draw the attention of the country in similar ways the O.J. Simpson trial did. Or, perhaps, like the more recent Florida trial of Casey Anthony accused of murdering her three-year-old daughter.

In both of those cases, the defendants were found "not guilty." Something troubling happened after the verdict was announced and the court room was emptied. Readers may recall that when the Simpson verdict was announced, groups of black people all over the country were shown dancing and partying, while Nicole Simpson's family (the victim's family) had to be physically carried from the courthouse in grief. We don't understand that kind of behavior. What does this say about us? Two people were gruesomely murdered. Have a little respect.

Similarly, Casey Anthony's defense team and friends held a party a stone's throw away from the courthouse following her "not guilty" verdict. They were toasting each other and bragging on how they were part of making history and how they made the law work in their favor. They laughed and congratulated each other while only steps away a prosecution team sat weeping because they felt they failed a little girl who also deserved some kind of justice.

No one wins in such cases. No one will win in George's trial. Trayvon is no longer with us, George is hated, his family uprooted and threatened daily. His life will never be the same regardless of the verdict. Neither will ours. Even though O.J. Simpson and Casey Anthony walked free, they are forever marked, identified, and convicted by a court of public opinion that was and is the final verdict no matter the findings of the Florida court.

If George has anything to say about it, there will no kind of celebration or party should he be found innocent. In our opinion, such displays are a travesty of the highest order. Perhaps a moment of silence would be fitting, or some kind of sober remembrance of a young man whose life was cut short regardless the reason. Maybe a prayer or appropriate comments offered in appreciation of our justice system, but please … no parties. I know that would be George's desire. But, we are far from any such possible moment. There is a lot of speculation as to when the trial will be underway, and then, how long it will last.

We are trying to prepare ourselves emotionally for a guilty verdict, but just can't seem to get there. It still seems so unlikely a jury would find George guilty of any criminal intent whatsoever. But, we also know we have a system of laws designed to administer justice, but sometimes gets it wrong because of the very parameters that attempt to make it fair to all.

In Dade North Memorial Park Cemetery, right off Interstate 95, close to Miami, a teenager was buried on March 3rd, six days after being shot. Trayvon Martin was buried in a white suit, with a light blue vest. Probably looked a lot like what he would have worn to the Junior Prom. We mourn his death as we would any young person's life cut short and we weep for all the broken hearts Trayvon left behind. This was an enormous tragedy.

On the same day, two hundred and fifty miles north in Lake Mary, Florida, our family locked the doors, made safety plans, and kept watch out our windows for any sign of danger. Every day, we held our friend, and cried with him and prayed for God's direction and protection. We asked ourselves after the first serious death threats were reported: *Are we in danger, too? Could our willingness to hide and protect George cost our own lives, or the life of our daughter?* The fear was real and indeed all those terrible things *were* possible during the month George and Shellie were in our home.

George struggled with the knowledge we might all come to harm if his presence became known. What we came to realize is that, for us, there was no other choice. Jesus said in John 15:13, "Greater love has no one than this; that he lay down his life for his friends." We were willing to risk our lives for our friend. We simply loved him that much.

Another verse from Proverbs 18 indicates a friendship which endures more strongly and loyally than even kinship by blood. These are friends who stick "closer than a brother." These are true, genuine friends. A person may have only one friend like that in a lifetime. That is who George Zimmerman is to us. We hope this message reaches him wherever he is. He may be one of the most hated men in America, but the Ostermans know the real George Zimmerman; a good man, a friend, a brother – no, someone closer than a brother whom we love and believe in. And, George, buddy – that's forever.

# Photo Section

Shellie and George Zimmerman with Breanna
Osterman at Breanna's Birthday Party

Breanna with Shellie Zimmerman and the Zimmermans' dog, Oso, at the beach

Shellie Zimmerman relaxing in their home at The Retreat at Twin Lakes where the shooting took place. Their dog, Oso, in forefront

George and Shellie with other friends, Bobby Williams and Jaime Vileg at Disney's Hollywood Studios, the Osbourne Lights Display. Breanna was in wheelchair temporarily due to Karate class injury

Sondra Osterman with daughter, Breanna at same Disney's event

# Postscript ...

A victory was scored by George's defense team a week after we taped the Dr. Phil show. On August 29th, Circuit Judge Kenneth Lester was disqualified as presiding judge over the upcoming trial. His successor has not been named as we go to print. Mark O'Mara, George's attorney presented a 28-page motion filled with reasons they didn't believe Lester would give George a fair trial. One of the reasons cited was that Lester had commented more than once that the state's case against George was "strong" and characterized Trayvon Martin as an unarmed juvenile, ignoring the evidence that George yelled for help for 40 seconds straight – during which time his nose was broken and his head was being pounded into the concrete.

There is no speculation as to when the 2nd degree murder trial will be underway. Until it is, George and Shellie Zimmerman are in a safe house somewhere in the country and remain in hiding.

# Special Thanks

We wanted to take this opportunity to say thank you to some very important people who have helped us throughout this life-changing journey. First and foremost we would like to give thanks to our Lord and Savior for guiding our family through some of the darkest days and for not only protecting our family, but also the Zimmerman family. Most of all, thank you Lord for sparing our friend George's life on the tragic night of February 26$^{th}$, 2012.

Next we'd like to thank everyone at Tate Publishing and Key Marketing Group for guiding us through this process and all your tireless work on this book, helping it be the best it could be. Rita Tate, Creative Project Director, "thank you" doesn't even almost cover the gratitude we have for you, but thank you for bringing our words to life and for putting up with the mountain of notes and questions and marathon phone calls. We appreciate you taking our passion for this project and making it your passion as well. You are a very gifted woman and we are so blessed to have been able to work with you all these months. God bless, we love you dearly. Also, sincere thanks to MJ Mock for research help and editing the manuscript.

Dr. Tate and Bryan Norris, thank you for believing in this project and for allowing our voice to be heard and for believing we had something to say. Thank you all for sharing our vision and giving us a platform to share The Real George Zimmerman with as many people as possible. You are all First Class!!!

To our parents, siblings and friends thank you all so much for your unconditional love and support. We are so blessed to have you all in our lives and have such an amazing support system. We know at times the stress on our parents was insurmountable, but we appreciate your confidence in our ability to take care of the situation at hand. Additionally, thank you for giving us the foundation to never back down from what we believe to be right even in the sight of danger. Your unwavering support for George and Shellie is priceless and much appreciated. We love you all.

To our daughter, Breanna Merri, thank you for bringing so much joy into our life each and every day. We pray that your love for people and life in general never changes. May God always guide you in life's ups and downs and help you to always stand for what you believe in. We love you, baby.

Lastly, George and Shellie, our love and support for both of you has no end. We pray that God will keep you both safe and restore your lives back to something that resembles what it was prior to February 26th, 2012. We hope you know this is our way of not allowing evil to triumph and we hope we resemble good men. We love you!!

—Mark and Sondra Osterman
August 2012

To purchase copies of this book, visit
www.tatepublishing.com

**TATE PUBLISHING**
AND ENTERPRISES, LLC